CODING
GAMES WITH
JAVASCRIPT

A Fun Approach to Learning JavaScript

THOMPSON CARTER

TABLE OF CONTENTS

INTRODUCTION

Coding Games with JavaScript: A Fun Approach to Learning JavaScript

Welcome to **Coding Games with JavaScript: A Fun Approach to Learning JavaScript**. Whether you're a beginner looking to dive into programming or someone who's familiar with the basics of JavaScript and wants to level up your skills, this book is designed to make the learning process both engaging and practical. By focusing on **game development** as the primary method of teaching, we aim to provide a hands-on, interactive approach to mastering JavaScript—one of the most popular programming languages in the world today.

Why JavaScript?

JavaScript has become the cornerstone of modern web development. It powers everything from interactive websites and web apps to mobile apps and games. Understanding JavaScript is essential for anyone who wants to build dynamic, user-friendly applications, and it's especially important for game development on the web.

Games, unlike traditional applications, have specific needs: real-time interactivity, smooth animations, sound integration, and logic-heavy mechanics. These are the areas where JavaScript excels, and this book will help you use its strengths to build fully functional, interactive games right in your browser.

Why Games?

You might wonder: **Why focus on games to teach JavaScript?**

The answer is simple: **Games are fun.**

Learning to code doesn't have to be tedious or abstract. By building games, you get to see the immediate impact of your code, and the process becomes interactive and rewarding. Each line of code directly contributes to the behavior and experience of the game. As you add new features, you'll see your progress unfold in real-time, and that constant feedback loop is one of the most effective ways to learn.

Games also integrate many important programming concepts such as **loops**, **conditionals**, **arrays**, **functions**, and **event handling**, all of which are core to mastering JavaScript. By focusing on game development, we'll show you how to apply these concepts in a concrete, enjoyable way.

What You'll Learn

Over the course of 24 chapters, you'll gradually build your knowledge of JavaScript, starting with the basics and progressing to more advanced concepts. Each chapter is designed to build on the previous one, with real-world examples and hands-on projects that will reinforce your understanding.

Here's a breakdown of the major skills you'll gain:

1. **Core JavaScript Fundamentals**: You'll learn the essential building blocks of JavaScript—variables, loops, conditionals, functions, and arrays—while writing simple games.

2. **User Interaction**: You'll master how to take input from users, process it, and trigger corresponding game actions, making your games responsive and interactive.

3. **Game Mechanics and Logic**: By building different types of games, you'll explore how to structure complex game mechanics, including scoring systems, timers, levels, and game progression.

4. **Animation and Graphics**: You'll dive into the world of animation with the HTML5 <canvas> element, learning to draw and animate shapes, characters, and backgrounds in your games.

5. **Object-Oriented Programming (OOP)**: You'll discover how to create reusable game objects using **classes** and **objects**, a key concept for organizing your code efficiently and making it easier to scale your projects.

6. **Sound and Music**: Adding sound to games makes them more immersive. You'll learn how to integrate sound effects and background music into your projects.

7. **Testing and Debugging**: You'll learn how to debug and test your code to make sure your games work smoothly, fixing errors and optimizing performance as you go.

8. **Game Design**: You'll also explore fundamental game design principles—like balancing difficulty, creating engaging challenges, and rewarding the player—all while keeping gameplay fun and accessible.

The Projects

This book isn't just about theory. It's about **building real games**. Each chapter features practical, step-by-step projects that teach you how to apply the concepts you learn to create interactive, playable games. These projects range from simple text-based games to more visually complex experiences, each carefully designed to challenge you in different ways.

For example, you'll start by creating a simple **guessing game**, which introduces basic concepts like variables, conditionals, and user input. As you progress, you'll create games with increasing complexity, such as a **bouncing ball game** using animations, a **memory matching game** with arrays and objects, and even a **platformer game** with character movement, gravity, and obstacles.

By the end of this book, you'll have built a fully functional **JavaScript game project**, demonstrating your ability to apply everything you've learned. This final project will be a reflection of your journey, showcasing your new skills while giving you the opportunity to experiment with your own ideas and creativity.

No Jargon, Just Fun Learning

One of the core philosophies of this book is to **keep things jargon-free**. JavaScript can be a dense language, but we aim to present it in a clear, easy-to-understand way. You won't be bombarded with complicated terms or theoretical explanations that go over your head. Instead, we'll guide you through practical examples and explanations, ensuring that everything is accessible, enjoyable, and—most importantly—fun.

We'll also take care to explain things in a way that avoids unnecessary complexity, while still providing depth and real-world context. If you ever feel stuck, you'll always have a project in front of you that demonstrates how things work in action.

What You Need

To get started, all you need is a basic text editor (like **VSCode** or **Sublime Text**) and a web browser (like **Chrome** or **Firefox**). We'll walk you through setting up your development environment in Chapter 1, so there's no need to worry about complicated software installations or configurations. Everything can be done directly in your browser, making it easy to start coding immediately.

Who This Book Is For

This book is for anyone who:

- Is new to programming and wants to learn JavaScript in an engaging, hands-on way.
- Has basic JavaScript knowledge but wants to learn how to apply it in the context of game development.
- Enjoys learning by doing, and wants to create interactive, fun projects while mastering coding concepts.
- Has a passion for games and wants to understand how to build them from scratch.

If you're someone who learns best by **building things** and wants to explore the world of game development, then this book is perfect for you.

Let's Get Started!

Now that you have an idea of what to expect, it's time to jump into the world of JavaScript game development. The skills you learn here are not just for building games—they'll help you with web development, app development, and even general programming logic. You'll gain experience that extends beyond the realm of gaming, preparing you to tackle more complex projects in the future.

So, let's get started! Turn the page, and let's begin building your first game. Happy coding!

CHAPTER 1: INTRODUCTION TO JAVASCRIPT AND GAME DEVELOPMENT

This chapter serves as the foundation of your journey into coding games with JavaScript. It provides a comprehensive overview of JavaScript, introduces basic game development concepts, and walks you through setting up your development environment. Let's break it down further:

---

1. Overview of JavaScript and Its Role in Web Development

What is JavaScript?

JavaScript is a dynamic, high-level programming language that powers interactivity on the web. It was originally developed by Netscape Communications in 1995 under the name "LiveScript" but was later renamed to JavaScript. Today, it is one of the core technologies of web development, alongside HTML and CSS.

- **Client-Side vs. Server-Side**: JavaScript traditionally operates on the *client-side*, which means it runs in the user's browser, allowing for things like form validation, dynamic content updates, and animations. More recently, JavaScript can also be used on the *server-side* via Node.js, allowing developers to build full-stack applications entirely in JavaScript.

- **Why JavaScript for Games?**
  - o **Universality**: Every modern web browser has a JavaScript engine, so you can build and play games on virtually any platform without installing additional software.
  - o **Performance**: While JavaScript isn't as fast as C++ or other lower-level languages used in game engines like Unity or Unreal, it's fast enough for 2D games and small to medium-sized projects, especially when paired with HTML5's <canvas> element for graphics rendering.
  - o **Libraries and Frameworks**: JavaScript has a rich ecosystem of libraries and tools (like Phaser.js) specifically tailored for game development, making it easier to create games without reinventing the wheel.

JavaScript's Versatility:

- **Frontend and Backend**: JavaScript is a full-stack language, meaning it can be used for both client-side and server-side development. On the front end, it interacts with HTML and CSS to create rich, interactive interfaces. On the back end, with Node.js, JavaScript can handle requests, manage databases, and serve dynamic content.

- **HTML5 + CSS + JavaScript**: This trio is the backbone of web development, and together they allow you to create interactive web pages. For games, HTML provides the structure, CSS is used for styling, and JavaScript adds interactivity.

- **JavaScript in Game Development**: With JavaScript, you can create interactive web-based games that are accessible to anyone with a web browser. It allows you to:
  - Control game flow and logic.
  - Handle user input (keyboard, mouse, or touch).
  - Create animations and visual effects.
  - Manage sounds and music in your games.

2. Brief Introduction to Game Development Principles

What is Game Development?

Game development is the process of creating video games, from concept to execution. It involves various disciplines, including design, programming, art, sound, and testing. When it comes to game development in JavaScript, you'll focus on the following core elements:

- **Gameplay Mechanics**: This refers to the rules and systems that govern how the game works. For example, if you're creating a platformer game, the mechanics might include jumping, moving, and avoiding obstacles.

- **Interactivity**: Games require continuous interaction between the player and the game world. In JavaScript, this is typically achieved through event listeners that track user input (e.g., mouse clicks, key presses) and trigger responses.

- **Graphics and Animation**: Visual elements, such as characters, backgrounds, and animations, are key to immersing the player in the game world. JavaScript allows you to draw and animate graphics on the screen using the HTML5 <canvas> element.

- **Sound**: Sound is an important part of the gaming experience, from background music to sound effects when actions occur (e.g., a jump, a collision, or a level up). JavaScript allows you to load and control sounds in your game.

Core Concepts of Game Development:

- **Game Loop**: A game loop is the heartbeat of a game. It continually updates the game state (position of objects, game logic, etc.) and renders the scene on the screen. In JavaScript, a game loop is typically implemented using requestAnimationFrame(), which ensures smooth animations and updates.

16

- **Game States**: Games often have multiple states—such as the main menu, the playing state, and the game over screen—that govern the flow of the game. JavaScript helps manage these states through conditionals and functions, allowing for smooth transitions between them.

- **Collision Detection**: For interactive games, detecting when objects collide (e.g., when a player's character hits an obstacle) is essential. In JavaScript, this involves using simple geometry (checking whether two objects overlap on the screen).

---

3. Setting Up Your Development Environment

Before writing any code, it's important to get your development environment ready. This ensures that you can write, test, and run your code efficiently.

Tools You'll Need:

1. **Text Editor/IDE**: A text editor is where you'll write your JavaScript code. There are many good editors available, but here are the top choices:
   - **Visual Studio Code**: A powerful, open-source code editor that supports JavaScript out of the box and has many extensions for game development.

o **Sublime Text**: Lightweight and fast, Sublime Text is also popular among web developers.

o **Atom**: Another popular, open-source text editor with a customizable interface.

These editors provide syntax highlighting, autocompletion, and debugging tools to make coding easier.

2. **Browser**: JavaScript runs in the browser, so it's important to test your code in a modern browser like:

o **Google Chrome**: Offers excellent developer tools for debugging JavaScript and inspecting the DOM.

o **Mozilla Firefox**: Great for testing compatibility and also has robust developer tools.

Browsers also allow you to view your game as it runs in real-time, making it easier to debug and improve your code.

Setting Up a Local Development Environment:

Here's a quick guide to setting up your project:

1. **Create a Folder for Your Game Project**:

o Make a new folder on your computer where all your game files will live. You might call it my-first-game.

2. **Create HTML and JavaScript Files**:

o Inside the folder, create an index.html file and a game.js file. The HTML file will hold the structure of your game (like the canvas element), and the JavaScript file will contain the game logic.

o Your folder should look like this:

perl

my-first-game/
├── index.html
├── game.js

3. **Write Your First HTML and JavaScript Code**:

o **HTML**: The index.html file will contain the basic structure of the web page and load the JavaScript.

html

```
<!DOCTYPE html>
<html lang="en">
<head>
    <meta charset="UTF-8">
    <meta name="viewport" content="width=device-width, initial-scale=1.0">
    <title>My First Game</title>
</head>
<body>
```

```html
<canvas        id="gameCanvas"        width="800"
height="600"></canvas>
    <script src="game.js"></script>
</body>
</html>
```

o **JavaScript**: In game.js, you'll start by selecting the canvas element and setting up your basic game loop.

javascript

```javascript
const            canvas            =
document.getElementById('gameCanvas');
const ctx = canvas.getContext('2d');

function gameLoop() {
    ctx.clearRect(0, 0, canvas.width, canvas.height);
// Clear the canvas
    ctx.fillStyle = 'blue';
    ctx.fillRect(50, 50, 100, 100);   // Draw a blue
square
    requestAnimationFrame(gameLoop);  // Keep the
game loop running
}

gameLoop(); // Start the game loop
```

4. **Testing Your Code**:

   o Open the index.html file in your web browser to view the game. You should see a blue square moving on a blank canvas.

   o Open the browser's developer tools (F12 in Chrome) to check for any errors in the console.

Installing Node.js (Optional for Advanced Users):

Node.js is not strictly necessary for building simple games with JavaScript in the browser, but it becomes essential if you plan to:

- Set up a development server.
- Work with JavaScript frameworks.
- Manage dependencies using npm (Node package manager).

To install Node.js:

1. Go to nodejs.org and download the latest stable version.
2. Follow the installation instructions based on your operating system.

Once installed, you can use the terminal to run JavaScript files and install game-related libraries.

In this chapter, we laid the groundwork for your JavaScript game development journey. We covered what JavaScript is, its role in web development, and why it's a great tool for building browser-based games. We also introduced fundamental game development principles and guided you through setting up your development environment, ensuring you're ready to start coding your first game.

In the next chapter, we'll dive into the basics of JavaScript syntax and build your first interactive game—an exciting step toward creating something tangible with the skills you're starting to learn!

CHAPTER 2: YOUR FIRST GAME: BUILDING A SIMPLE GUESSING GAME

In this chapter, you'll write your very first JavaScript game: a simple guessing game where the user has to guess a random number between 1 and 100. This game will introduce you to some key concepts in JavaScript, such as variables, functions, conditionals, and handling user input. By the end of this chapter, you'll have the foundation for creating interactive games with logic, input, and feedback.

---

1. Basic JavaScript Syntax: Variables, Functions, and Conditionals

Before we dive into the guessing game, let's review the core building blocks of JavaScript that we'll be using.

Variables

Variables are containers for storing data. You can assign values to variables using the let, const, or var keywords. In modern JavaScript, let and const are preferred over var for block-level scoping.

- let is used when the value of the variable may change.
- const is used when the value should not change.

Example:

javascript

```
let userGuess = 0;  // The variable to store the user's guess
const maxNumber = 100;  // The maximum number for the guessing range
```

Functions

A function is a block of reusable code that performs a specific task. Functions are defined using the function keyword.

Example:

javascript

```
function showMessage(message) {
    alert(message);  // Display a message in an alert box
}
```

Conditionals (if/else)

Conditionals allow you to make decisions in your code based on whether a condition is true or false. The most common conditional structure in JavaScript is the if statement.

Example:

javascript

```
if (userGuess === correctNumber) {
    alert("Congratulations, you guessed correctly!");
} else {
    alert("Try again!");
}
```

---

2. User Input with Prompts and Alerts

In a guessing game, you'll need to collect user input (the guess) and provide feedback (whether the guess is too high, too low, or correct). JavaScript provides two simple methods to interact with the user: prompt() and alert().

prompt()

The prompt() method displays a dialog box that asks the user for input. It returns the input as a string.

Example:

javascript

```
let userGuess = prompt("Guess a number between 1 and 100:");
```

This will display a prompt asking the user to enter a guess.

alert()

The alert() method displays a message in a dialog box. It's a simple way to communicate with the user.

Example:

javascript

alert("You guessed: " + userGuess);

---

3. Setting Up an Interactive Game with Simple Logic

Now that we have a basic understanding of JavaScript syntax, let's put it all together by building the guessing game.

The game will work as follows:

1. The computer generates a random number between 1 and 100.
2. The player is asked to guess the number using a prompt.
3. The game will tell the player whether the guess was too high, too low, or correct.
4. The game will keep asking for guesses until the player guesses correctly.

Let's write the code for this game step by step.

Step 1: Generate a Random Number

We'll use JavaScript's Math.random() function to generate a random number between 1 and 100.

javascript

```javascript
// Generate a random number between 1 and 100
const correctNumber = Math.floor(Math.random() * 100) + 1;
```

- Math.random() generates a random number between 0 (inclusive) and 1 (exclusive).
- Math.floor() rounds the number down to the nearest integer.
- Multiplying by 100 gives a number between 0 and 99, and adding 1 ensures that the number is between 1 and 100.

Step 2: Collect User Input

Next, we'll ask the player to guess the number using the prompt() method.

javascript

```javascript
let userGuess = parseInt(prompt("Guess a number between 1 and 100:"));
```

- parseInt() is used to convert the string input from the prompt into an integer.

Step 3: Provide Feedback (Using Conditionals)

We'll use an if statement to compare the user's guess to the correct number and give feedback.

javascript

```javascript
if (userGuess === correctNumber) {
    alert("Congratulations! You guessed the number correctly.");
} else if (userGuess < correctNumber) {
    alert("Your guess is too low. Try again.");
} else {
    alert("Your guess is too high. Try again.");
}
```

This will provide the player with feedback on whether their guess was too high, too low, or correct.

Step 4: Repeating the Game

To make the game interactive, we'll need to loop the game until the user guesses the correct number. We can achieve this using a while loop that continues asking for input until the guess is correct.

javascript

```javascript
let userGuess = 0;  // Initialize the guess variable
const correctNumber = Math.floor(Math.random() * 100) + 1;  // Generate the random number

while (userGuess !== correctNumber) {
    userGuess = parseInt(prompt("Guess a number between 1 and 100:"));
```

```javascript
if (userGuess === correctNumber) {
    alert("Congratulations! You guessed the number correctly.");
} else if (userGuess < correctNumber) {
    alert("Your guess is too low. Try again.");
} else {
    alert("Your guess is too high. Try again.");
}
}
```

Here's what happens:

- The while loop continues to prompt the user until their guess equals the correctNumber.
- Each time the user guesses, the game provides feedback via alert().

Full Code Example:

Now, let's look at the complete code for the guessing game.

javascript

```javascript
// Generate a random number between 1 and 100
const correctNumber = Math.floor(Math.random() * 100) + 1;


let userGuess = 0; // Initialize the guess variable
```

```
// Start the game loop
while (userGuess !== correctNumber) {
    // Ask the player to guess a number
    userGuess = parseInt(prompt("Guess a number between 1 and 100:"));


    // Check if the guess is correct, too high, or too low
    if (userGuess === correctNumber) {
        alert("Congratulations! You guessed the number correctly.");
    } else if (userGuess < correctNumber) {
        alert("Your guess is too low. Try again.");
    } else {
        alert("Your guess is too high. Try again.");
    }
}
```

In this chapter, you've learned how to:

1. **Use variables** to store data, such as the user's guess and the correct number.
2. **Define functions** to encapsulate reusable logic (e.g., checking if the guess is correct).

3. **Use conditionals** (if, else if, else) to compare the user's guess with the correct number and provide feedback.

4. **Collect user input** with prompt() and give feedback with alert().

5. **Repeat a game loop** using a while loop to continue prompting the user until they guess correctly.

You've now built a simple but fully functional guessing game, which can be expanded with additional features like keeping track of the number of attempts or providing hints.

In the next chapter, we'll start to explore more interactive elements, such as using keyboard events, and move into more complex game mechanics.

CHAPTER 3: VARIABLES, LOOPS, AND LOGIC: ESSENTIAL BUILDING BLOCKS

In this chapter, we'll explore three key programming concepts that are foundational to game development: **variables**, **loops**, and **logic**. By understanding these building blocks, you'll be able to create more complex and interactive games. Specifically, you'll learn about different **data types** in JavaScript, how to use **loops** for repetitive tasks, and how to apply **logic** to build a basic text-based adventure game.

1. Understanding Different Data Types in JavaScript

In JavaScript, data types define what kind of value a variable can hold. Understanding these types is essential because it influences how you can manipulate, store, and compare data.

Primitive Data Types:

JavaScript has several primitive data types, which are the most basic types of data you'll work with.

- **String**: A sequence of characters. Used for text.
  - o Example:

javascript

```
let name = "Alice";
let description = "You are in a dark forest.";
```

- **Number**: Represents both integer and floating-point numbers (decimals).
  - o Example:

  javascript

  ```
  let playerHealth = 100;
  let playerScore = 256.75;
  ```

- **Boolean**: A type that has two possible values: true or false. Used for logical operations.
  - o Example:

  javascript

  ```
  let hasKey = true;
  let isGameOver = false;
  ```

- **Null**: Represents the intentional absence of any value or object.
  - o Example:

javascript

```
let playerInventory = null;  // No items in inventory yet.
```

- **Undefined**: A variable that has been declared but has not yet been assigned a value.
    - Example:

javascript

```
let currentWeapon;   // Undefined, since it's not assigned a value yet.
```

Objects and Arrays:

- **Object**: A collection of key-value pairs. It's often used to store complex data structures.
    - Example:

javascript

```
let player = {
   name: "Alice",
   health: 100,
   inventory: ["sword", "shield"]
};
```

- **Array**: A list of values (can be of any type), stored in a single variable.

  - Example:

    javascript

    let enemies = ["goblin", "orc", "dragon"];

2. Introduction to Loops and How They Work

Loops are essential when you need to repeat a block of code multiple times. They are particularly useful in games for tasks such as checking the player's status, repeating actions, or cycling through a list of items or enemies.

For Loop:

A for loop runs a block of code a specific number of times. It's commonly used when you know in advance how many iterations are needed.

Syntax:

javascript

```
for (let i = 0; i < 10; i++) {
    console.log(i);  // Will print numbers from 0 to 9
}
```

In game development, a for loop can be used to cycle through a list of enemies or levels.

Example:

javascript

```javascript
for (let i = 0; i < enemies.length; i++) {
    console.log("You face a " + enemies[i]);
}
```

While Loop:

A while loop runs as long as a specified condition is true. It's useful when you don't know how many iterations are needed ahead of time.

Syntax:

javascript

```javascript
let playerHealth = 100;
while (playerHealth > 0) {
    console.log("You have " + playerHealth + " health remaining.");
    playerHealth -= 10;  // Decrease health by 10 after each loop
}
```

In games, while loops are useful for checking conditions like the player's health or whether the game should continue.

Do-While Loop:

A do-while loop guarantees that the code runs at least once, as the condition is checked after the loop is executed.

Syntax:

javascript

```
let choice;
do {
    choice = prompt("Do you want to continue? (yes/no)");
} while (choice === "yes");
```

In a game, a do-while loop could repeatedly prompt the player for input until they provide a valid response.

---

3. Building a Basic Text-Based Adventure Game

Now that we have covered the basics of variables, data types, and loops, let's put them to use by building a simple text-based adventure game. In this game, the player will navigate through a series of rooms and make decisions that will affect the outcome of the story.

Game Concept:

The game will consist of the player navigating through different rooms in a dungeon. The player can choose to go left or right, and each choice will lead to a different outcome (e.g., encounter an enemy, find a treasure, or reach the exit).

Step 1: Set Up the Game State

We'll use variables to keep track of the player's health, inventory, and current location.

javascript

```
let playerHealth = 100;
let inventory = [];
let currentRoom = "start";  // The player starts in the 'start' room
```

Step 2: Define the Game Logic

We will use a while loop to keep the game running until the player either loses all their health or exits the dungeon.

javascript

```
while (playerHealth > 0 && currentRoom !== "exit") {
  if (currentRoom === "start") {
    let choice = prompt("You are in a dark room. Do you want to go left or right?");

    if (choice === "left") {
      currentRoom = "enemy";
    } else if (choice === "right") {
      currentRoom = "treasure";
    } else {
      alert("Invalid choice. Please type 'left' or 'right'.");
    }
  }
```

```
if (currentRoom === "enemy") {
    alert("A wild goblin appears!");
    let action = prompt("Do you want to fight or run?");

    if (action === "fight") {
        let fightResult = Math.random();
        if (fightResult < 0.5) {
            alert("You defeated the goblin!");
            currentRoom = "start";  // Return to the start room after defeating the goblin
        } else {
            alert("You were defeated by the goblin.");
            playerHealth = 0;  // Player loses the game if they lose the fight
        }
    } else if (action === "run") {
        alert("You escaped the goblin.");
        currentRoom = "start";  // Return to the start room after running away
    }
}

if (currentRoom === "treasure") {
    alert("You find a treasure chest!");
    let action = prompt("Do you want to open the chest? (yes/no)");
```

```
    if (action === "yes") {
        inventory.push("gold coin");
        alert("You found a gold coin! Your inventory: " +
inventory.join(", "));
        currentRoom = "start";   // Return to the start room after
opening the chest
    } else {
        alert("You decided not to open the chest.");
        currentRoom = "start";   // Return to the start room if the
player chooses not to open the chest
    }
  }
}


if (playerHealth <= 0) {
    alert("Game Over! You have been defeated.");
} else if (currentRoom === "exit") {
    alert("Congratulations! You escaped the dungeon.");
}
```

Step 3: Game Flow

- The game starts in the "start" room.
- The player can choose to go left or right.

- If they go left, they encounter an enemy; if they go right, they find a treasure.
- Depending on their choices, the player may either fight the enemy, escape, or collect items from the treasure chest.
- The game continues until the player either loses all their health or escapes the dungeon.

In this chapter, we covered some essential building blocks for JavaScript game development:

1. **Variables and Data Types**: Understanding how to store different types of data (strings, numbers, booleans, etc.) and how to use them in your game.
2. **Loops**: Learning how to use for, while, and do-while loops to repeat actions or check conditions during gameplay.
3. **Building a Text-Based Adventure Game**: Putting it all together to create an interactive text-based game where the player can make decisions that affect the outcome.

In the next chapter, we'll dive into more advanced game mechanics, such as handling player input using the keyboard and improving game flow.

CHAPTER 4: HANDLING USER INPUT: THE BACKBONE OF INTERACTIVE GAMES

In this chapter, we'll focus on handling **user input** —a crucial aspect of interactive game development. We'll explore how to gather information from the player, provide feedback, and create dynamic experiences based on user choices. By the end of the chapter, you'll know how to use JavaScript methods like prompt(), alert(), and confirm() to create engaging decision-making games.

---

1. Using prompt(), alert(), and confirm()

JavaScript provides several built-in methods to interact with users: prompt(), alert(), and confirm(). These methods allow you to capture input, display messages, and ask for confirmation in a simple, straightforward way.

prompt()

The prompt() method is used to get user input through a dialog box that appears in the browser. It takes a string argument that serves as the message or question to the user. It returns the input as a string (or null if the user cancels).

Syntax:

javascript

```javascript
let userInput = prompt("What is your name?");
```

Example:

javascript

```javascript
let playerName = prompt("Enter your name:");
alert("Welcome, " + playerName + "!");
```

- **Use Case**: Gathering user input, such as names, choices, or answers to questions.

alert()

The alert() method displays a message in a dialog box to the user. It is typically used for showing notifications or feedback. After the user clicks "OK," the program resumes.

Syntax:

javascript

```javascript
alert("You have completed the level!");
```

Example:

javascript

```javascript
let health = 50;
```

```javascript
if (health <= 0) {
    alert("Game Over! You have been defeated.");
}
```

- **Use Case**: Displaying messages, such as success, failure, or status updates.

confirm()

The confirm() method displays a dialog box with a message and "OK" and "Cancel" buttons. It returns a boolean value (true if "OK" is clicked, false if "Cancel" is clicked). This is useful when you need a user to confirm or reject an action, such as quitting the game or making an important decision.

Syntax:

javascript

```javascript
let result = confirm("Are you sure you want to quit?");
```
Example:

javascript

```javascript
let choice = confirm("Do you want to attack the dragon?");
if (choice) {
    alert("You attack the dragon!");
} else {
```

```
alert("You decide to run away.");
}
```

- **Use Case**: Asking the user for a yes/no decision, like confirming actions or options.

---

2. *Creating Interactive Prompts for User Choices*

In game development, interactivity is key. You'll often need to ask the player to make choices that affect the outcome of the game. By using prompt() and confirm(), you can allow users to make decisions and interact with the story.

Let's create a simple decision-making game using these methods.

Example Game: Choose Your Path

In this game, the player will make decisions that affect their fate. The game will present different paths, and the player's choices will lead to different scenarios.

javascript

```
// Starting point
let playerHealth = 100;
let playerName = prompt("What is your name?");
alert("Welcome to the adventure, " + playerName + "!");
```

CODING GAMES WITH JAVASCRIPT

```javascript
// First choice
let firstChoice = prompt("You are standing at a fork in the road. Do you go left or right?");

if (firstChoice.toLowerCase() === "left") {
    // Path to encounter
    alert("You chose the left path.");
    let encounter = confirm("You encounter a wild wolf! Do you want to fight?");

    if (encounter) {
        let fightResult = Math.random();
        if (fightResult > 0.5) {
            alert("You defeated the wolf!");
            playerHealth -= 10;  // Decrease health after the fight
        } else {
            alert("The wolf defeated you.");
            playerHealth = 0;  // Player loses if defeated
        }
    } else {
        alert("You ran away from the wolf safely.");
    }
} else if (firstChoice.toLowerCase() === "right") {
    // Path to treasure
    alert("You chose the right path.");
```

```
    let treasure = confirm("You find a treasure chest. Do you want to
open it?");

    if (treasure) {
        alert("You open the chest and find gold and a healing potion!");
        playerHealth += 20;  // Heal the player
    } else {
        alert("You decide not to open the chest and move on.");
    }
} else {
    alert("Invalid choice. You must choose 'left' or 'right'.");
}

if (playerHealth <= 0) {
    alert("Game Over! You have no health left.");
} else {
    alert("You continue your journey with " + playerHealth + "
health.");
}
```

Game Flow Explanation:

1. The player enters their name.
2. The player faces a decision to go left or right.
3. If the player goes left, they encounter a wolf and are given a choice to fight or run.

4. If the player goes right, they find a treasure chest and are given the choice to open it.

5. Depending on their choices, their health may increase or decrease.

6. The game continues based on the player's remaining health.

Key Concepts:

- The prompt() method is used to gather the player's initial input and decisions.

- The confirm() method allows the player to make critical yes/no choices (e.g., fighting or running, opening a treasure chest).

- Conditional logic (using if and else) controls the flow of the game, directing the player based on their choices.

---

3. Building a Decision-Making Game

Now that you understand how to collect user input and create interactive prompts, let's take a deeper dive into building a more structured decision-making game. We'll structure the game around a series of challenges, where the player's decisions lead to different outcomes. The focus will be on managing the flow of the game based on user input, and incorporating the concepts learned so far.

Example Game: The Quest for the Crystal

In this example, the player is on a quest to find a magical crystal. They'll need to make decisions that will affect their survival, their inventory, and ultimately whether they succeed or fail in the quest.

javascript

```javascript
let playerName = prompt("Welcome to the Quest for the Crystal. What is your name?");
alert("Good luck, " + playerName + "!");

let health = 100;
let inventory = [];
let questComplete = false;

// First decision: entering the forest
let enterForest = confirm("Do you want to enter the dark forest?");

if (enterForest) {
    alert("You enter the dark forest...");
    let pathChoice = prompt("You come to a fork in the road. Do you take the left path or the right path?");

    if (pathChoice.toLowerCase() === "left") {
        // Encounter with a creature
        let fightChoice = confirm("A wild beast appears! Do you want to fight?");
```

```javascript
    if (fightChoice) {
        let fightOutcome = Math.random();
        if (fightOutcome > 0.4) {
            alert("You defeated the beast!");
            health -= 20;  // Damage from the fight
            inventory.push("beast's claw");
        } else {
            alert("The beast overpowers you.");
            health = 0;  // Player loses if defeated
        }
    } else {
        alert("You ran away from the beast, but you lost some health in the process.");
        health -= 10;  // Running away costs health
    }
} else if (pathChoice.toLowerCase() === "right") {
    // Finding the crystal
    alert("You find the magical crystal! You've completed your quest.");
    questComplete = true;
} else {
    alert("Invalid choice. You stand still in confusion.");
}
} else {
    alert("You decide to turn back and not enter the forest.");
```

```
}

// End of the game
if (health <= 0) {
    alert("Game Over! You have no health left.");
} else if (questComplete) {
    alert("Congratulations! You have successfully completed the
quest!");
} else {
    alert("You leave the forest and return home, with " + health + "
health remaining.");
}
```

Game Flow Explanation:

1. The player starts by entering their name.
2. The player is prompted to enter a forest. If they choose yes, they are presented with a fork in the road.
3. Depending on the path they choose, they may encounter a creature, where they can either fight or run.
4. If they defeat the creature, they gain an item (beast's claw), but lose some health. Running away results in a smaller health loss.
5. If they take the right path, they immediately find the crystal and complete the quest.

6. The game ends based on the player's remaining health or whether they complete the quest.

In this chapter, we covered the essential techniques for handling user input in interactive games:

1. **Using prompt(), alert(), and confirm()**: These methods provide the basic tools for gathering input, providing feedback, and asking the player to make decisions.

2. **Creating Interactive Prompts**: By using conditional logic, we can create branching storylines and decision-making points, where the player's choices

CHAPTER 5: THE POWER OF FUNCTIONS: SIMPLIFYING YOUR CODE

In this chapter, we'll explore the concept of **functions**—one of the most powerful and essential tools in programming. Functions allow you to encapsulate reusable logic, making your code more organized, efficient, and easier to maintain. Functions are especially valuable in game development, where repetitive tasks (like calculations or user input handling) need to be done multiple times. We'll also look at how to use **parameters** to pass information into functions, and finally, we'll build a simple **calculator game** to demonstrate these concepts in action.

---

1. Introduction to Functions and Parameters

A **function** is a block of reusable code that performs a specific task. Once defined, you can call (or invoke) the function anywhere in your program, saving you from repeating the same code. Functions can take **parameters**, which are values passed into the function when it is called, allowing it to work with different data each time it runs.

Function Syntax:

javascript

```
function functionName(parameters) {
    // Code to be executed
}
```

- **functionName**: The name you assign to the function.
- **parameters**: Variables that act as placeholders for values you pass into the function when you call it. Parameters are optional—if no parameters are needed, the function can be written without them.

Example of a Simple Function:

javascript

```
function greet(name) {
    alert("Hello, " + name + "!");
}
```

```
greet("Alice");   // Calls the function and passes "Alice" as the argument
greet("Bob");     // Calls the function and passes "Bob" as the argument
```

In this example, the greet function takes one parameter (name) and displays a greeting message. The parameter allows the function to be flexible, working with any name passed to it.

2. How Functions Help in Organizing Your Game Code

When building games, there are often repeated tasks or complex operations that need to be done multiple times. Functions help **organize** your code by grouping related operations together. Instead of writing the same code over and over, you define a function once and call it whenever you need it. This leads to cleaner, more efficient, and easier-to-maintain code.

Benefits of Functions in Game Development:

- **Code Reusability**: Functions allow you to reuse the same code multiple times. For example, a function for calculating damage or checking the player's health can be used in different parts of the game.

- **Separation of Concerns**: Functions allow you to break down complex tasks into smaller, more manageable chunks. For example, instead of writing out the entire game logic in one giant block, you can divide it into functions like attack(), defend(), heal(), etc.

- **Clarity and Maintainability**: Functions make your code more readable and modular. If a part of your game isn't working, it's easier to locate and fix bugs when each task is neatly contained within its own function.

Example: Organizing Game Code with Functions

Let's take the **health-checking logic** from our previous game example and turn it into a reusable function.

javascript

```javascript
function checkHealth(health) {
    if (health <= 0) {
        alert("Game Over! You have no health left.");
        return false;  // Game over if health is 0 or below
    }
    return true;  // Continue the game if health is above 0
}


// Example usage in the game flow:
let playerHealth = 100;


playerHealth -= 20;  // Player loses health after a fight
if (!checkHealth(playerHealth)) {
    // End the game if health is 0
} else {
    alert("You have " + playerHealth + " health remaining.");
}
```

Here, the checkHealth() function is a modular piece of code that can be reused whenever we need to check the player's health, making the main game logic cleaner and more manageable.

3. Building a Calculator Game with User Input

Now, let's put the power of functions and parameters to practical use by building a **calculator game**. The player will be asked to solve simple math problems, and the game will check whether their answer is correct.

Step 1: Define Functions for Operations

We'll start by creating separate functions for each mathematical operation (addition, subtraction, multiplication, division).

javascript

```javascript
// Function for addition
function add(a, b) {
    return a + b;
}


// Function for subtraction
function subtract(a, b) {
    return a - b;
}


// Function for multiplication
function multiply(a, b) {
    return a * b;
```

```
}
```

```
// Function for division
function divide(a, b) {
    if (b === 0) {
        alert("Cannot divide by zero!");
        return null;  // Return null if dividing by zero
    }
    return a / b;
}
```

Each of these functions takes two parameters (a and b), performs the operation, and returns the result.

Step 2: Building the Game Flow

Now, let's use the functions to create an interactive game. The player will be asked a series of math questions, and the game will check if their answers are correct.

javascript

```
function askQuestion(question, correctAnswer) {
    let playerAnswer = prompt(question);
    if (parseInt(playerAnswer) === correctAnswer) {
        alert("Correct!");
        return true;  // Player answered correctly
    } else {
```

```
    alert("Wrong  answer.  The  correct  answer  was  " +
correctAnswer);
    return false; // Player answered incorrectly
  }
}


// Main game flow
let score = 0;

let question1 = "What is 3 + 4?";
let correctAnswer1 = add(3, 4);  // Call the 'add' function to get the
correct answer
if (askQuestion(question1, correctAnswer1)) {
    score++;
}


let question2 = "What is 10 - 6?";
let correctAnswer2 = subtract(10, 6);  // Call the 'subtract' function
to get the correct answer
if (askQuestion(question2, correctAnswer2)) {
    score++;
}


let question3 = "What is 5 * 2?";
```

```
let correctAnswer3 = multiply(5, 2);  // Call the 'multiply' function
to get the correct answer
if (askQuestion(question3, correctAnswer3)) {
    score++;
}


let question4 = "What is 20 / 4?";
let correctAnswer4 = divide(20, 4);  // Call the 'divide' function to
get the correct answer
if (askQuestion(question4, correctAnswer4)) {
    score++;
}


alert("Your final score is " + score + "/4.");
```

Game Flow Explanation:

1. The game starts by initializing the score to 0.
2. The player is presented with a series of math questions (addition, subtraction, multiplication, division).
3. For each question, the corresponding function is called to calculate the correct answer.
4. The player's input is checked against the correct answer, and the score is updated accordingly.
5. At the end of the game, the player's final score is displayed.

Key Concepts in This Example:

- We created multiple **functions** to handle different operations (add, subtract, multiply, divide).
- The **askQuestion()** function handles the interaction with the player, taking the question and correct answer as arguments, and comparing the player's input.
- Functions are used to **simplify** and **organize** the code, making it easier to add more questions or operations in the future.

In this chapter, we explored the power of **functions** and how they can help organize and simplify your game code. Key takeaways include:

1. **Functions** allow you to bundle reusable logic into a single unit, reducing code duplication.
2. **Parameters** let you customize a function's behavior by passing different values into it when the function is called.
3. **Organizing Game Code**: Functions help keep your code clean and modular, making it easier to maintain and expand.
4. **Building a Calculator Game**: We applied these concepts by building a simple interactive calculator game where the player answers math questions.

In the next chapter, we'll explore **arrays** and how they can help you manage collections of data, like inventories or enemy lists, in your games.

CHAPTER 6: ARRAYS AND OBJECTS: STORING GAME DATA

In this chapter, we'll dive into the powerful data structures that JavaScript offers: **arrays** and **objects**. These two structures are essential for storing and managing **game data**, which could include things like player stats, high scores, choices made during the game, or even game assets like images or sounds. By the end of the chapter, you'll know how to use arrays and objects to efficiently store and manipulate data, and we'll build a **memory matching game** as a practical example to demonstrate how these structures are used.

1. Using Arrays and Objects to Manage Game Data

Arrays in JavaScript

An **array** is a list-like data structure that can hold multiple values. You can store any type of data in an array, including numbers, strings, or even other arrays and objects. Arrays are perfect for situations where you need to keep track of multiple items, such as **scores**, **player choices**, or **game assets**.

- **Array Syntax:**

javascript

```
let myArray = [element1, element2, element3, ...];
```

- **Accessing Array Elements**: You can access array elements using their **index** (remember, arrays are 0-indexed).

javascript

```
let scores = [10, 20, 30, 40];
console.log(scores[0]);  // Output: 10
```

- **Common Array Methods**:
  - push(): Adds an element to the end of the array.
  - pop(): Removes the last element from the array.
  - shift(): Removes the first element.
  - unshift(): Adds an element to the beginning of the array.
  - forEach(): Loops through each element in the array.

Objects in JavaScript

An **object** is a more flexible data structure that allows you to store data as **key-value pairs**. This is useful for storing more complex data, like **player stats**, **game settings**, or **character attributes**.

- **Object Syntax**:

javascript

```
let player = {
  name: "Alice",
```

```
  health: 100,
  score: 0,
  level: 1
};
```

- **Accessing Object Properties**: You can access properties using dot notation or bracket notation.

javascript

```
console.log(player.name);  // Output: Alice
console.log(player["score"]);  // Output: 0
```

- **Adding/Modifying Properties**:

javascript

```
player.health = 90;  // Modify an existing property
player.inventory = ["sword", "shield"];  // Add a new property
```

- **Common Object Methods**: While objects don't have the same built-in methods as arrays, you can still manipulate them by writing your own functions or using Object.keys() and Object.values() to loop through their properties.

---

2. Storing Scores, Player Stats, and Choices

Arrays and objects are extremely useful for managing **game data** like **scores**, **player stats**, and **choices**. Here's how you might use them to organize and store this information:

Storing High Scores with Arrays

In many games, you'll want to store and track **high scores**. An array is perfect for this task.

javascript

```
let highScores = [500, 450, 400, 350, 300];  // Example high scores
```

```
// Adding a new score
let newScore = 475;
highScores.push(newScore);  // Add the new score to the end of the array
```

```
// Sorting scores in descending order
highScores.sort((a, b) => b - a);
console.log(highScores);  // Output: [500, 475, 450, 400, 350]
```

Here, we've used an array to track high scores and sorted them in descending order. If you wanted to add a mechanism to display the top 5 scores, this approach would work well.

Storing Player Stats with Objects

For storing more detailed information about the player, such as their **health**, **level**, **score**, and **inventory**, you can use an object.

javascript

```
let playerStats = {
    name: "Alice",
    health: 100,
    score: 0,
    level: 1,
    inventory: ["sword", "shield"]
};
```

```
// Modifying stats during the game
playerStats.score += 50;  // Add 50 to the score
playerStats.health -= 20;  // Subtract 20 from the health
```

```
console.log(playerStats);   // Output: { name: 'Alice', health: 80,
score: 50, level: 1, inventory: [ 'sword', 'shield' ] }
```

This object allows you to store various attributes related to the player's progress in the game. You can also add more complex structures as needed, like **quests** or **abilities**.

Tracking Player Choices with Arrays

Sometimes, you'll want to keep track of the **choices** the player makes throughout the game. This can be achieved using an array.

javascript

let playerChoices = []; // Array to store the player's decisions

// During the game, you push choices into the array
playerChoices.push("Chose to fight the dragon");
playerChoices.push("Saved the princess");
playerChoices.push("Looted the treasure chest");

console.log(playerChoices); // Output: ['Chose to fight the dragon', 'Saved the princess', 'Looted the treasure chest']

Arrays are a great way to store sequential information like choices or events in the order they happen.

---

3. Creating a Memory Game (Matching Pairs)

Now, let's use **arrays** and **objects** to build a simple **memory game** where the player needs to match pairs of cards. In this game, the cards will be represented by pairs of objects, and we'll store the game's state (e.g., the cards the player has flipped) in an array.

Step 1: Representing the Cards with Objects

Each card in the memory game will be an object with a name (e.g., the card's value) and a flipped status (whether the card has been flipped over).

javascript

```javascript
let cards = [
    { name: "A", flipped: false },
    { name: "A", flipped: false },
    { name: "B", flipped: false },
    { name: "B", flipped: false },
    { name: "C", flipped: false },
    { name: "C", flipped: false }
];
```

Step 2: Shuffling the Cards

We need to shuffle the cards so they aren't in a predictable order.

javascript

```javascript
function shuffleArray(array) {
    for (let i = array.length - 1; i > 0; i--) {
        const j = Math.floor(Math.random() * (i + 1));
        [array[i], array[j]] = [array[j], array[i]];  // Swap elements
    }
    return array;
}
```

```javascript
cards = shuffleArray(cards);
console.log(cards);  // Output: shuffled array of card objects
```

Step 3: Implementing the Game Logic

Let's implement the game logic, where the player flips over two cards at a time and tries to match them.

javascript

```javascript
let flippedCards = []; // Array to store flipped cards

function flipCard(index) {
    if (cards[index].flipped) {
        console.log("Card already flipped.");
        return;
    }

    cards[index].flipped = true;
    flippedCards.push(cards[index]);

    console.log(`Flipped: ${cards[index].name}`);

    // Check if two cards are flipped
    if (flippedCards.length === 2) {
        checkMatch();
    }
}

function checkMatch() {
    if (flippedCards[0].name === flippedCards[1].name) {
```

70

```
        console.log("It's a match!");
    } else {
        console.log("Not a match. Try again.");
        // Reset flipped cards after a short delay
        setTimeout(() => {
            flippedCards[0].flipped = false;
            flippedCards[1].flipped = false;
            flippedCards = [];
        }, 1000);
    }
}
```

Step 4: Playing the Game

The player can call the flipCard() function to flip a card and check for matches. The game checks whether the two flipped cards match, and if they do, they remain flipped; otherwise, they're turned back over.

javascript

```
flipCard(0);  // Flip the first card
flipCard(1);  // Flip the second card
flipCard(2);  // Flip the third card
```

In this chapter, we covered how to use **arrays** and **objects** to efficiently manage and store **game data**. Key takeaways include:

1. **Arrays** are useful for storing lists of data, like scores, player choices, or game assets.

2. **Objects** are ideal for storing related data as key-value pairs, like player stats, character attributes, or game settings.

3. We used arrays and objects to build a simple **memory game**, where the player flips over cards and tries to match pairs.

In the next chapter, we'll explore **game loops** and **animations**, which are crucial for creating smooth and interactive game experiences.

CHAPTER 7: BASIC ANIMATION: MOVING OBJECTS ON THE SCREEN

In this chapter, we'll dive into the exciting world of **animation** in JavaScript by introducing the **HTML5 <canvas> element**. This element provides a space in the browser where we can draw graphics and create animations using JavaScript. By the end of this chapter, you will understand how to use JavaScript to animate shapes on the screen and build a **simple bouncing ball game** as a practical example.

---

1. Introduction to the HTML5 <canvas> Element

The **<canvas>** element is a powerful feature introduced in HTML5 that allows you to draw graphics on a web page using JavaScript. It provides a **drawing surface** for creating shapes, images, and animations. The <canvas> itself is an empty container, and you use JavaScript to manipulate the drawing context within it.

Canvas Syntax:

html

```
<canvas id="gameCanvas" width="500" height="500"></canvas>
```

- **id="gameCanvas"**: The ID allows us to reference the canvas element in our JavaScript.
- **width and height**: Specifies the size of the canvas in pixels.

To draw on the canvas, we first need to **access the 2D drawing context** via JavaScript. The context provides methods and properties for drawing shapes, lines, and text.

Getting the 2D Context:

javascript

```javascript
let canvas = document.getElementById("gameCanvas");
let ctx = canvas.getContext("2d");
```

- **getContext("2d")**: This method returns a 2D drawing context that lets you draw 2D shapes, paths, and images.

---

2. Using JavaScript to Draw Shapes and Animate Them

Once you have the canvas and context, you can begin drawing shapes like **rectangles**, **circles**, and **lines**.

Drawing Basic Shapes:

1. **Drawing a Rectangle**:

javascript

```
ctx.fillStyle = "blue";  // Set the fill color
ctx.fillRect(50, 50, 100, 100);  // Draw a filled rectangle at (50, 50)
```
with width 100 and height 100

2. **Drawing a Circle**:

javascript

```
ctx.beginPath();  // Begin a new path
ctx.arc(200, 200, 50, 0, Math.PI * 2);  // Draw a circle with center
(200, 200) and radius 50
ctx.fillStyle = "green";  // Set the fill color
ctx.fill();  // Fill the circle with the chosen color
```

3. **Drawing Text**:

javascript

```
ctx.font = "20px Arial";  // Set the font size and family
ctx.fillStyle = "red";  // Set the text color
ctx.fillText("Hello, world!", 150, 150);  // Draw text at (150, 150)
```

Animating Shapes:

To animate shapes, we use a combination of **requestAnimationFrame()** and the clearRect() method to clear the canvas before drawing new frames. **requestAnimationFrame()** is a browser API that helps create smooth animations by calling a function repeatedly at the optimal frame rate.

The typical animation loop looks like this:

1. **Clear the canvas** at the start of each frame.
2. **Draw the shapes** in new positions.
3. **Request the next frame** using requestAnimationFrame().

Basic Animation Example:

Let's animate a **ball** that moves across the canvas.

javascript

```
let canvas = document.getElementById("gameCanvas");
let ctx = canvas.getContext("2d");

// Ball properties
let ballRadius = 20;
let x = canvas.width / 2;
let y = canvas.height - ballRadius - 30;
let dx = 2;  // Speed of the ball in the x direction
let dy = -2;  // Speed of the ball in the y direction

// Draw the ball
function drawBall() {
    ctx.beginPath();
```

```
    ctx.arc(x, y, ballRadius, 0, Math.PI * 2);
    ctx.fillStyle = "#0095DD";
    ctx.fill();
    ctx.closePath();
}


// Update the ball's position and animate
function draw() {
    ctx.clearRect(0, 0, canvas.width, canvas.height);   // Clear the
canvas

    drawBall();  // Redraw the ball

    // Update ball position
    x += dx;
    y += dy;

    // Bounce off the walls
    if (x + dx > canvas.width - ballRadius || x + dx < ballRadius) {
        dx = -dx;
    }
    if (y + dy > canvas.height - ballRadius || y + dy < ballRadius) {
        dy = -dy;
    }
```

```
// Call draw() again for the next frame
requestAnimationFrame(draw);
}
```

```
// Start the animation
draw();
```

Explanation of the Code:

1. **drawBall()**: This function draws the ball at its current position (x, y).

2. **draw()**: This function is the **game loop** that updates the ball's position and redraws it on the canvas. It also checks for boundary collisions and makes the ball bounce when it hits the edges.

3. **requestAnimationFrame(draw)**: This ensures that the draw() function is called repeatedly, creating a smooth animation.

---

3. Building a Simple Bouncing Ball Game

Now that you understand how to animate shapes on the canvas, let's take it a step further by building a **bouncing ball game** where the player controls a paddle to bounce the ball and prevent it from falling off the screen. This will introduce you to **user input handling** and basic game logic.

Step 1: Set Up Game Elements

We'll need:

- A **ball** (already created).
- A **paddle** that the player can move left and right using the arrow keys.

javascript

```
let paddleHeight = 10;
let paddleWidth = 75;
let paddleX = (canvas.width - paddleWidth) / 2;
let rightPressed = false;
let leftPressed = false;

// Draw the paddle
function drawPaddle() {
    ctx.beginPath();
    ctx.rect(paddleX, canvas.height - paddleHeight, paddleWidth,
paddleHeight);
    ctx.fillStyle = "#0095DD";
    ctx.fill();
    ctx.closePath();
}
```

Step 2: Handle User Input (Keyboard Events)

We need to listen for **keyboard events** to move the paddle. The **keydown** event will be used to move the paddle left and right, and the **keyup** event will stop the paddle when the keys are released.

javascript

```
// Key event listeners
document.addEventListener("keydown", keyDownHandler, false);
document.addEventListener("keyup", keyUpHandler, false);

function keyDownHandler(e) {
    if (e.key == "Right" || e.key == "ArrowRight") {
        rightPressed = true;
    } else if (e.key == "Left" || e.key == "ArrowLeft") {
        leftPressed = true;
    }
}

function keyUpHandler(e) {
    if (e.key == "Right" || e.key == "ArrowRight") {
        rightPressed = false;
    } else if (e.key == "Left" || e.key == "ArrowLeft") {
        leftPressed = false;
    }
}
```

Step 3: Move the Paddle

In the draw() function, update the position of the paddle based on user input.

javascript

```
function draw() {
    ctx.clearRect(0, 0, canvas.width, canvas.height);   // Clear the canvas

    drawBall();  // Redraw the ball
    drawPaddle();  // Redraw the paddle

    // Move the paddle based on user input
    if (rightPressed && paddleX < canvas.width - paddleWidth) {
        paddleX += 7;  // Move paddle right
    } else if (leftPressed && paddleX > 0) {
        paddleX -= 7;  // Move paddle left
    }

    // Ball movement and boundary checks (same as before)
    x += dx;
    y += dy;

    if (x + dx > canvas.width - ballRadius || x + dx < ballRadius) {
        dx = -dx;
```

```
    }
    if (y + dy > canvas.height - ballRadius) {
        if (x > paddleX && x < paddleX + paddleWidth) {
            dy = -dy;  // Ball hits the paddle
        } else {
            // Game Over condition (ball falls off the screen)
            alert("GAME OVER");
            document.location.reload();
        }
    } else if (y + dy < ballRadius) {
        dy = -dy;  // Ball hits the top of the canvas
    }


    requestAnimationFrame(draw);  // Request the next frame
}


draw(); // Start the game
```

Game Flow Explanation:

1. The **ball** moves around the canvas, bouncing off the edges.
2. The player controls the **paddle** using the arrow keys.
3. If the ball hits the paddle, it bounces back. If it falls off the bottom of the screen (i.e., the player misses it), the game ends with a **Game Over** alert.

In this chapter, we covered the basics of **animation** using the HTML5 <canvas> element and JavaScript. Key takeaways include:

1. **HTML5 <canvas>** is used to draw and animate shapes on the screen.
2. We learned how to draw basic shapes (rectangles, circles) and animate them using **requestAnimationFrame()** for smooth animations.
3. We built a **bouncing ball game** with a paddle controlled by the user and explored simple **collision detection**.

In the next chapter, we'll explore **game physics**, where we'll introduce more complex mechanics like gravity, velocity, and friction to make the game more realistic.

CHAPTER 8: EVENTS AND LISTENERS: MAKING GAMES RESPONSIVE

In this chapter, we will explore the core concept of **events** in JavaScript and how to use **event listeners** to make our games responsive to player input. By the end of this chapter, you'll learn how to detect different types of events, such as mouse clicks and keyboard presses, and create a simple **click-based game** like "Click the Button" to win. This game will serve as a foundation for understanding how to make games interactive and dynamic.

---

1. Understanding Events in JavaScript: Click, Keydown, etc.

In JavaScript, an **event** is an action that occurs in the system you are interacting with, such as a user clicking a button, pressing a key, or moving the mouse. Events are a key part of interactive applications like games, as they allow your game to respond to user input.

Common Event Types:

1. **Click Events** (click): Triggered when the user clicks on an element (e.g., a button, image, or any clickable object).
2. **Keyboard Events** (keydown, keyup, keypress): Triggered when the user presses a key on the keyboard.

    o **keydown**: Fired when a key is pressed down.

    o **keyup**: Fired when a key is released.

3. **Mouse Events** (mousemove, mousedown, mouseup): Triggered by mouse actions.

4. **Touch Events** (touchstart, touchmove, touchend): Triggered by touch events on mobile devices.

For a game, the most commonly used events are **click events** for interaction and **keydown/keyup** events for controlling movement or actions.

Event Syntax:

To make an event happen, you first need to listen for the event and then respond to it. You can achieve this using **event listeners**.

javascript

```
// Example of a click event listener
document.getElementById("myButton").addEventListener("click",
function() {
    alert("Button clicked!");
});
```

In this example:

- **addEventListener()** attaches an event handler to the myButton element.

- The **click** event is fired when the user clicks the button, and the anonymous function is executed, showing an alert.

---

2. Event Listeners for Player Input

Event listeners are the bridge between the player's actions and the game's response. In games, event listeners are used to capture player input (e.g., clicking on objects, pressing keys to move characters, etc.) and trigger specific game actions based on that input.

Setting Up Event Listeners:

Let's look at how we can use event listeners to capture different types of player input and trigger game-related actions.

1. **Click Event for Button Interaction**: For example, we can use a button element to trigger some game action when clicked.

html

```html
<button id="startButton">Start Game</button>
```

javascript

```javascript
let startButton = document.getElementById("startButton");

startButton.addEventListener("click", function() {
```

```javascript
alert("Game Started!");
// Start game logic here
});
```

2. **Keyboard Event for Player Movement**: For player movement or actions triggered by keyboard input (like moving a character), you can use the **keydown** event to detect when a key is pressed.

javascript

```javascript
document.addEventListener("keydown", function(event) {
    if (event.key === "ArrowLeft") {
        console.log("Move left");
    } else if (event.key === "ArrowRight") {
        console.log("Move right");
    }
});
```

In this case, the player can use the **left** or **right arrow keys** to trigger specific movement actions.

3. **Mouse Events for Game Interaction**: Mouse events like **click**, **mousedown**, or **mousemove** can be used to trigger game actions when the player interacts with the game using their mouse.

javascript

```javascript
document.getElementById("gameCanvas").addEventListener("click", function(event) {
    let x = event.clientX;  // Get the mouse's x-coordinate
    let y = event.clientY;  // Get the mouse's y-coordinate
    console.log(`Mouse clicked at (${x}, ${y})`);
});
```

This event listener listens for **mouse clicks** on the gameCanvas, and it logs the mouse coordinates where the click occurred.

---

3. Creating a Click-Based Game: "Click the Button" to Win

Now that we understand how to use event listeners, let's apply this knowledge by building a simple **click-based game** where the player needs to click a button to win the game. The objective is for the player to click the button as many times as possible in a given time limit, and the number of clicks will be counted.

Step 1: Setting Up the Game Structure

We'll need a button the player can click, a timer to count down, and a display to show the score.

html

```html
<!DOCTYPE html>
```

```html
<html lang="en">
<head>
  <meta charset="UTF-8">
  <meta name="viewport" content="width=device-width, initial-scale=1.0">
  <title>Click the Button Game</title>
</head>
<body>
  <h1>Click the Button to Win!</h1>
  <p>Time left: <span id="timer">10</span> seconds</p>
  <p>Score: <span id="score">0</span></p>
  <button id="clickButton">Click Me!</button>

  <script src="game.js"></script>
</body>
</html>
```

Step 2: Writing the JavaScript Logic

1. **Initialize the Game**: Set up variables for **score** and **time left**.
2. **Start the Timer**: Use setInterval to update the timer and count down.
3. **Count Clicks**: Use an event listener for the **click** event to increment the score.
4. **End the Game**: Stop the game when the timer reaches 0.

javascript

```javascript
// Game variables
let score = 0;
let timeLeft = 10;  // 10 seconds timer
let scoreDisplay = document.getElementById("score");
let timerDisplay = document.getElementById("timer");
let clickButton = document.getElementById("clickButton");

// Start the game
function startGame() {
    // Reset the score and time
    score = 0;
    timeLeft = 10;
    scoreDisplay.textContent = score;
    timerDisplay.textContent = timeLeft;

    // Timer countdown
    let timerInterval = setInterval(function() {
        timeLeft--;
        timerDisplay.textContent = timeLeft;
        if (timeLeft <= 0) {
            clearInterval(timerInterval);  // Stop the timer
            alert("Game Over! Your score is: " + score);
        }
```

```
}, 1000);


// Event listener for button clicks
clickButton.addEventListener("click", function() {
    score++;  // Increment the score each time the button is clicked
    scoreDisplay.textContent = score;
});
}


// Start the game when the page loads
window.onload = function() {
    startGame();
};
```

How the Game Works:

1. When the page loads, the **startGame()** function is called, initializing the score to 0 and starting the 10-second timer.
2. Every time the player clicks the **"Click Me!"** button, the **score** increases by 1.
3. The **timer** counts down every second. When it reaches 0, the game stops, and the player is alerted with their score.

In this chapter, we explored the concept of **events** in JavaScript and how to make our games **responsive** to user input through **event listeners**. Key takeaways include:

1. **Events** capture player actions (clicks, key presses, mouse movements) and trigger corresponding functions in the game.
2. **Event listeners** are used to "listen" for events and respond with specific game actions, such as moving a character, increasing the score, or stopping a timer.
3. We created a simple **click-based game** ("Click the Button to Win"), where the player clicks a button to accumulate points within a time limit.

In the next chapter, we will look into more advanced **game mechanics** such as **collision detection** and how to detect when objects in the game world interact with each other.

CHAPTER 9: WORKING WITH TIMERS: ADDING TIME TO YOUR GAMES

Timers are an essential component of many games. They can create a sense of **urgency**, **count down to an event**, or simply control the timing of game actions. In this chapter, we'll learn how to use **setTimeout()** and **setInterval()** in JavaScript to add timed events to your games. We'll also build a **countdown timer** for a **quiz game** to give you a practical example of how timers work in a game context. This chapter will focus on introducing **time-based game mechanics** that can enhance the overall gaming experience.

---

1. Using setTimeout() and setInterval() for Timed Events

JavaScript provides two key functions for managing timed events:

1. **setTimeout()**: Executes a function or code snippet after a specified delay (in milliseconds). It's a one-time timer that will run once after the specified time has passed.

   Syntax:

   javascript

setTimeout(function, delay);

- o **function**: The function to be executed after the delay.
- o **delay**: The time (in milliseconds) to wait before the function is executed.

Example:

javascript

```
setTimeout(function() {
    alert("Time's up!");
}, 5000); // Will show the alert after 5 seconds
```

2. **setInterval()**: Executes a function repeatedly at specified intervals. It runs at the defined interval until **clearInterval()** is called.

Syntax:

javascript

```
setInterval(function, interval);
```

- o **function**: The function to be executed at regular intervals.
- o **interval**: The time (in milliseconds) between each execution.

Example:

javascript

```
let counter = 0;
let intervalId = setInterval(function() {
    console.log("Seconds passed: " + counter);
    counter++;
}, 1000);  // Logs every second

// To stop the interval after 10 seconds
setTimeout(function() {
    clearInterval(intervalId);
}, 10000);
```

In this example, the setInterval() function runs every second and logs the count. After 10 seconds, clearInterval() is called to stop the interval.

---

2. Building a Countdown Timer for a Quiz Game

Now, let's put these timer functions to use by building a **countdown timer** for a **quiz game**. The player will have a limited amount of time to answer each question, and when the timer runs out, their answer will be automatically submitted or the game will end.

Step 1: Setting Up the HTML Structure

We need the following elements:

- A countdown timer to display the remaining time.
- A question to answer.
- A set of possible answers (buttons, for example).

html

```
<!DOCTYPE html>
<html lang="en">
<head>
  <meta charset="UTF-8">
  <meta name="viewport" content="width=device-width, initial-scale=1.0">
  <title>Quiz Game</title>
</head>
<body>
  <h1>Quiz Time!</h1>
  <p id="question">What is the capital of France?</p>
  <button id="answer1">Berlin</button>
  <button id="answer2">Madrid</button>
  <button id="answer3">Paris</button>
  <button id="answer4">London</button>
  <p>Time left: <span id="timer">30</span> seconds</p>

  <script src="quiz.js"></script>
```

```
</body>
</html>
```

Step 2: Writing the JavaScript Logic

1. **Start the Countdown**: Use setInterval() to count down the timer each second.
2. **Handle Answer Choices**: When the player selects an answer, stop the timer and check if the answer is correct.
3. **Game Over**: If the timer reaches 0, automatically submit the answer.

javascript

```javascript
// Game variables
let timerDisplay = document.getElementById("timer");
let questionDisplay = document.getElementById("question");
let answerButtons = document.querySelectorAll("button");
let timeLeft = 30;  // 30 seconds to answer

// Timer countdown function
let countdown = setInterval(function() {
    timeLeft--;
    timerDisplay.textContent = timeLeft;

    if (timeLeft <= 0) {
```

```
      clearInterval(countdown);  // Stop the timer
      alert("Time's up! The correct answer was: Paris.");
      gameOver();

   }
}, 1000);


// Handle answer button clicks
answerButtons.forEach(function(button) {
   button.addEventListener("click", function() {
      clearInterval(countdown);  // Stop the timer when the player
clicks an answer
      let answer = button.textContent;
      if (answer === "Paris") {
         alert("Correct! Well done.");
      } else {
         alert("Wrong answer! The correct answer was: Paris.");
      }
      gameOver();
   });
});


// Game over function
function gameOver() {
   questionDisplay.textContent = "Game Over!";
   answerButtons.forEach(function(button) {
```

```
    button.disabled = true;  // Disable all answer buttons
  });
}
```

How the Quiz Game Works:

1. **Countdown**: The timer starts at 30 seconds and counts down every second using setInterval(). When the timer reaches 0, the game ends.

2. **Answer Selection**: When the player clicks one of the answer buttons, the timer stops, and the game checks if the answer is correct.

3. **Game Over**: Once the timer runs out or the player selects an answer, the game displays a "Game Over" message, disables the answer buttons, and stops the game.

---

3. Adding Urgency to Your Game Mechanics

In games, **urgency** can be a powerful motivator, making players feel pressure and excitement. By using **timed events** effectively, you can create a sense of urgency that influences how the player interacts with the game. Here are some ideas for adding urgency:

1. **Time-Based Challenges**:
   - Create levels where players must complete tasks or puzzles within a set time.

- For example, in a maze game, the player must escape before the time runs out, or in a trivia game, they must answer correctly within a time limit.

2. **Limited-Time Power-Ups**:
   - Use timers to make power-ups last for a limited time, forcing the player to act quickly while they have the advantage.

3. **Time Penalties**:
   - For every wrong answer or failed action, deduct time from the player's countdown, adding more challenge to the game.

4. **Time-Bound High Scores**:
   - Display the player's score relative to how much time was left, encouraging faster performance. Players can compete to see who can score the highest within a limited time.

In this chapter, we learned how to use **timers** to create **time-based game mechanics** that add urgency and challenge to your games. Key concepts include:

1. **setTimeout()** and **setInterval()** are used to execute functions after a delay or at regular intervals, respectively.

2. **Countdown Timers**: We built a quiz game with a countdown timer, where the player has a limited amount of time to answer a question.

3. **Adding Urgency**: Timers can increase the sense of urgency in your game, encouraging faster decision-making and adding excitement.

In the next chapter, we'll explore **collision detection** and how objects in your game world interact with each other, allowing us to build more complex game mechanics.

CHAPTER 10: RANDOMNESS IN GAMES: GENERATING RANDOM NUMBERS

Randomness plays a crucial role in many games, adding unpredictability and excitement. Whether it's generating random enemies, items, or events, random elements keep players on their toes and enhance the gaming experience. In this chapter, we'll dive into the use of **Math.random()** in JavaScript to introduce **randomization** into our games. By the end of this chapter, you will learn how to use random numbers to create games that feel dynamic and unpredictable.

---

1. Using Math.random() for Randomization

JavaScript's built-in **Math.random()** function is used to generate random floating-point numbers between 0 (inclusive) and 1 (exclusive). This is the foundation for generating randomness in your game logic.

How Math.random() Works:

- **Math.random()** returns a number between **0** and **1** (but never reaching 1).
- For example:

javascript

```
let randomNumber = Math.random();
console.log(randomNumber);   // A random number like 0.2345
```

However, for game purposes, you usually need random numbers within a specific range (e.g., between 1 and 100, or randomly picking one out of multiple options). Let's see how to transform Math.random() for more specific use cases.

Generating Random Integers in a Range:

To generate a random integer within a specific range (e.g., between 1 and 100), we can scale and round the value returned by Math.random().

javascript

```
function getRandomInt(min, max) {
   return Math.floor(Math.random() * (max - min + 1)) + min;
}
```

- **Math.floor()** rounds down the floating-point number to the nearest whole number.
- **(max - min + 1)** ensures the number is inclusive of the max value.

For example, to generate a random integer between 1 and 100:

javascript

```
let randomNum = getRandomInt(1, 100);
console.log(randomNum);  // A random number between 1 and 100
```

Generating Random Floats in a Range:

If you need a floating-point number in a specific range, you can use:

javascript

```
function getRandomFloat(min, max) {
    return Math.random() * (max - min) + min;
}
```

This will return a **floating-point number** between min and max.

---

2. Creating a Random Number Guessing Game

Now that we understand how to generate random numbers, let's create a **random number guessing game**, where the player has to guess a randomly generated number within a given range.

Step 1: Setting Up the HTML Structure

We need the following elements:

- An input box to let the player enter their guess.
- A button to submit the guess.

- A display area to show whether the guess was correct or too high/low.

html

```
<!DOCTYPE html>
<html lang="en">
<head>
  <meta charset="UTF-8">
  <meta name="viewport" content="width=device-width, initial-scale=1.0">
  <title>Number Guessing Game</title>
</head>
<body>
  <h1>Guess the Number!</h1>
  <p>I'm thinking of a number between 1 and 100.</p>
  <input type="number" id="guessInput" placeholder="Enter your guess" />
  <button id="submitGuess">Submit Guess</button>
  <p id="feedback"></p>

  <script src="game.js"></script>
</body>
</html>
```

Step 2: Writing the JavaScript Logic

1. **Generate a Random Number**: Use getRandomInt(1, 100) to generate a secret number between 1 and 100.

2. **Capture User Input**: Use an input field where the player can type their guess.

3. **Compare Guess to Secret Number**: Check whether the guess is correct, too high, or too low.

4. **Provide Feedback**: Display messages to guide the player.

javascript

```javascript
let secretNumber = getRandomInt(1, 100);  // Generate a random number between 1 and 100
let guessInput = document.getElementById("guessInput");
let submitButton = document.getElementById("submitGuess");
let feedbackDisplay = document.getElementById("feedback");

submitButton.addEventListener("click", function() {
    let playerGuess = parseInt(guessInput.value);

    if (playerGuess === secretNumber) {
        feedbackDisplay.textContent = "Congratulations! You guessed the correct number!";
    } else if (playerGuess < secretNumber) {
        feedbackDisplay.textContent = "Too low! Try again.";
    } else if (playerGuess > secretNumber) {
```

```
    feedbackDisplay.textContent = "Too high! Try again.";
  }
});
```

```
// Helper function to generate random integers
function getRandomInt(min, max) {
  return Math.floor(Math.random() * (max - min + 1)) + min;
}
```

How the Game Works:

1. The game generates a **random secret number** between 1 and 100 when the page loads.
2. The player enters a guess into the input field and clicks the **"Submit Guess"** button.
3. The game compares the guess with the secret number and provides feedback: "Too low", "Too high", or "Correct!"
4. The game will continue allowing the player to guess until they find the right number.

---

3. Generating Random Events in a Text-Based Game

Random events can add excitement and variety to a game, especially in **text-based adventures**. For example, in a simple **dungeon crawler** or **role-playing game (RPG)**, you can generate random events like encountering a monster, finding an item, or triggering a trap.

Step 1: Setting Up a Basic Text-Based Game

In a text-based game, the player can move through different scenarios, and each scenario can trigger a random event. We'll build a simple version of this concept.

html

```html
<!DOCTYPE html>
<html lang="en">
<head>
  <meta charset="UTF-8">
  <meta name="viewport" content="width=device-width, initial-scale=1.0">
  <title>Random Event RPG</title>
</head>
<body>
  <h1>Dungeon Adventure!</h1>
  <p>You're in a dark dungeon. What will you do?</p>
  <button id="explore">Explore</button>
  <p id="eventMessage"></p>

  <script src="game.js"></script>
</body>
```

```
</html>
```

Step 2: Writing the JavaScript for Random Events

In this example, every time the player clicks **"Explore"**, the game generates a random event, such as encountering a monster, finding gold, or stepping into a trap.

javascript

```javascript
let exploreButton = document.getElementById("explore");
let eventMessage = document.getElementById("eventMessage");

exploreButton.addEventListener("click", function() {
    let event = getRandomInt(1, 3);  // Random number between 1 and 3 to choose the event

    if (event === 1) {
        eventMessage.textContent = "You encountered a wild monster! Prepare for battle!";
    } else if (event === 2) {
        eventMessage.textContent = "You found a hidden stash of gold! (+50 Gold)";
    } else if (event === 3) {
        eventMessage.textContent = "You stepped on a trap! Lose 10 health.";
    }
```

```
});


// Helper function to generate random integers
function getRandomInt(min, max) {
    return Math.floor(Math.random() * (max - min + 1)) + min;
}
```

How the Text-Based RPG Works:

1. The player clicks the **"Explore"** button to explore the dungeon.
2. A random number between 1 and 3 is generated, determining the outcome:
   - **1**: The player encounters a monster.
   - **2**: The player finds gold.
   - **3**: The player steps on a trap.
3. The result is displayed on the screen, and the game logic can be expanded to include more events or consequences.

In this chapter, we explored how to introduce **randomness** into your games using JavaScript's **Math.random()** function. Key takeaways include:

1. **Math.random()** generates random numbers between 0 and 1, which can be scaled and manipulated to create random values within specific ranges.

2. We built a **random number guessing game**, where the player tries to guess a randomly generated number.

3. We created a **text-based RPG** that generates random events (such as encountering a monster or finding gold) every time the player clicks the "Explore" button.

In the next chapter, we'll look at **game loops** and how to keep your games running continuously, handling updates like animations, physics, and player actions in real-time.

CHAPTER 11: GAME LOOPS AND LOGIC: KEEPING THE GAME RUNNING SMOOTHLY

A **game loop** is the heart of most games, enabling continuous updates to the game world and user input, and ensuring everything runs smoothly and at the correct speed. Whether it's moving objects, checking for collisions, or updating scores, a game loop runs repeatedly, handling all the game's logic in real-time. In this chapter, we'll explore how to set up a **game loop** in JavaScript and make use of **requestAnimationFrame()** to improve performance, and build a basic moving object game—such as a **snake** or **spaceship**—to demonstrate these concepts.

---

1. Understanding the Game Loop and Continuous Updates

In traditional game development, the **game loop** is a cycle that continuously runs to update the game's state and render frames. The loop performs several critical functions:

- **Handling user input**: Detecting key presses or mouse clicks.
- **Updating game state**: Moving objects, calculating physics, and checking collisions.
- **Rendering**: Redrawing the game scene to display the updated state.

Here's a simplified view of a game loop:

1. **Initialize** game state (variables, objects).
2. **Update** the game state (e.g., move objects, check for collisions).
3. **Render** the updated game scene.
4. **Repeat** the process.

In a typical game, you want the game loop to run **continuously** at a consistent frame rate, like 60 frames per second (FPS). This ensures smooth animation and responsiveness.

Basic Game Loop (without requestAnimationFrame()):

javascript

```javascript
let lastTime = 0;

function gameLoop(timestamp) {
    // Calculate the time elapsed between frames
    let deltaTime = timestamp - lastTime;
    lastTime = timestamp;

    update(deltaTime);  // Update game state
    render();         // Draw the game scene

    requestAnimationFrame(gameLoop);  // Request the next frame
```

```
}

function update(deltaTime) {
    // Update positions, game logic, etc.
    console.log("Updating game state with deltaTime: " + deltaTime);
}

function render() {
    // Clear the screen and redraw game objects
    console.log("Rendering game objects.");
}

// Start the game loop
requestAnimationFrame(gameLoop);
```

The **requestAnimationFrame()** function ensures that the game loop runs at an optimal frame rate by syncing with the browser's refresh rate. It is more efficient than using setInterval() or setTimeout() for continuous updates because it runs only when the browser is ready to paint a new frame.

---

2. Introduction to requestAnimationFrame()

requestAnimationFrame() is a built-in JavaScript function that optimizes the timing of your game's animation and game loop.

Unlike setInterval() and setTimeout(), which can cause choppy animations or lag, requestAnimationFrame():

- Syncs the game's update and rendering cycle with the browser's refresh rate (usually 60 FPS).
- Helps save resources by pausing animation when the game is not visible (e.g., when the user switches tabs).
- Reduces unnecessary calculations and screen redraws, leading to better performance.

How requestAnimationFrame() Works:

- It takes a function as an argument and schedules that function to be executed before the next repaint.
- The function receives a **timestamp** as an argument, which is the time when the frame is drawn.

Example:

javascript

```javascript
function gameLoop(timestamp) {
    // Game loop logic here
    // `timestamp` helps track time for animations or movement
    updateGame();
    renderGame();
    requestAnimationFrame(gameLoop);  // Request the next frame
```

}

requestAnimationFrame(gameLoop);

The **timestamp** is passed automatically to the callback, and it can be used to calculate the elapsed time between frames, which is useful for smooth animations and physics.

---

3. Creating a Moving Object Game (Snake or Spaceship)

Now, let's apply these concepts by creating a simple game where an object moves across the screen. We'll start by building a basic **spaceship** that moves with the arrow keys, simulating the logic of a game loop.

Step 1: HTML Structure

We need a basic HTML structure with a <canvas> element to display the game.

html

```
<!DOCTYPE html>
<html lang="en">
<head>
    <meta charset="UTF-8">
    <meta name="viewport" content="width=device-width, initial-scale=1.0">
```

```
<title>Spaceship Game</title>
<style>
  body {
    margin: 0;
    overflow: hidden;
  }
  canvas {
    display: block;
    background-color: #000;
  }
</style>
</head>
<body>
  <canvas id="gameCanvas"></canvas>

  <script src="game.js"></script>
</body>
</html>
```

Step 2: JavaScript Logic (Spaceship Game)

1. **Set Up the Canvas**: The canvas is where we'll draw our
   spaceship.
2. **Create the Game Loop**: Using requestAnimationFrame(),
   we'll continuously update the game state and render it to the
   screen.

3. **Move the Spaceship**: The spaceship will move according to the arrow keys.

javascript

```
// Set up the canvas and context
let canvas = document.getElementById("gameCanvas");
let ctx = canvas.getContext("2d");

// Set canvas size
canvas.width = window.innerWidth;
canvas.height = window.innerHeight;

// Spaceship object
let spaceship = {
    x: canvas.width / 2,
    y: canvas.height / 2,
    width: 50,
    height: 50,
    speed: 5,
    dx: 0, // movement in x direction
    dy: 0  // movement in y direction
};

// Handle keyboard input
```

```
let keys = {
    ArrowUp: false,
    ArrowDown: false,
    ArrowLeft: false,
    ArrowRight: false
};

document.addEventListener("keydown", function(event) {
    if (event.key in keys) {
        keys[event.key] = true;
    }
});

document.addEventListener("keyup", function(event) {
    if (event.key in keys) {
        keys[event.key] = false;
    }
});

// Update spaceship position based on input
function updateGame() {
    // Move spaceship based on arrow keys
    if (keys.ArrowUp) spaceship.dy = -spaceship.speed;
    if (keys.ArrowDown) spaceship.dy = spaceship.speed;
    if (keys.ArrowLeft) spaceship.dx = -spaceship.speed;
```

```javascript
    if (keys.ArrowRight) spaceship.dx = spaceship.speed;

    // Update spaceship position
    spaceship.x += spaceship.dx;
    spaceship.y += spaceship.dy;

    // Prevent spaceship from going out of bounds
    if (spaceship.x < 0) spaceship.x = 0;
    if (spaceship.x + spaceship.width > canvas.width) spaceship.x =
canvas.width - spaceship.width;
    if (spaceship.y < 0) spaceship.y = 0;
    if (spaceship.y + spaceship.height > canvas.height) spaceship.y =
canvas.height - spaceship.height;

    // Reset speed for smooth movement
    spaceship.dx = 0;
    spaceship.dy = 0;
}

// Render game objects
function renderGame() {
    // Clear the canvas
    ctx.clearRect(0, 0, canvas.width, canvas.height);

    // Draw the spaceship
```

```
ctx.fillStyle = "white";
ctx.fillRect(spaceship.x,      spaceship.y,      spaceship.width,
spaceship.height);
}


// Main game loop
function gameLoop(timestamp) {
    updateGame();   // Update game state
    renderGame();   // Render updated game state
    requestAnimationFrame(gameLoop);   // Request the next frame
}


// Start the game loop
requestAnimationFrame(gameLoop);
```

How the Game Works:

1. **Spaceship Movement**: The spaceship moves in response to the arrow keys. When an arrow key is pressed, the spaceship's direction changes, and it moves in the corresponding direction.
2. **Game Loop**: The gameLoop() function is called continuously using requestAnimationFrame(). It calls updateGame() to update the spaceship's position and renderGame() to draw the updated spaceship.

3. **Canvas**: The game is rendered on the <canvas>, which is cleared and redrawn on each frame.

In this chapter, we learned how to set up a **game loop** using **requestAnimationFrame()** to ensure smooth, continuous game updates and animations. Key takeaways include:

1. **Game Loop**: The game loop continuously updates the game state and renders the updated scene.

2. **requestAnimationFrame()**: This method helps synchronize the game loop with the browser's refresh rate, providing better performance and smoother animations.

3. **Moving Objects**: We demonstrated creating a **spaceship game** where the spaceship moves in response to arrow keys, all handled by the game loop.

In the next chapter, we'll dive deeper into **collision detection** and how to handle interactions between objects in your game world.

CHAPTER 12: IMPROVING THE USER INTERFACE: MAKING GAMES MORE ENGAGING

User Interface (UI) design is an essential part of game development. The UI serves as the bridge between the player and the game, making the experience more immersive, engaging, and intuitive. Whether it's a **start screen**, a **game over screen**, or just adding basic interactivity through **buttons** and **images**, improving the UI can elevate the overall gaming experience.

In this chapter, we will explore how to enhance the UI for your games by working with **HTML elements**, styling with **CSS**, and adding key features like **start screens** and **game over screens**. We'll build upon the previous spaceship game to demonstrate these concepts.

---

1. Working with HTML Elements (Buttons, Images, etc.)

In any game, the player will need some basic UI elements to interact with the game, such as buttons to start the game, images for visual appeal, and text to display important information (like scores, instructions, or game over messages). Let's begin by adding a **start screen** and **game over screen** to the spaceship game.

Start Screen:

The start screen should provide the player with a way to begin the game. We will create a **"Start Game"** button, which the player can click to launch the game.

Game Over Screen:

After the player loses (e.g., the spaceship crashes or a specific condition is met), we need a screen to inform them that the game is over, along with an option to **restart** or **exit**.

---

2. Styling the Game Interface with CSS

Good styling helps create an appealing and immersive game experience. We'll use CSS to create visually engaging screens. This includes:

- **Centering content** on the page (like the game title, buttons, and instructions).
- Styling the **start button** and **game over screen** for visibility and interaction.

Let's start by modifying the HTML and adding some CSS for basic styling.

HTML Structure (Updated with Start and Game Over Screens)

html

```
<!DOCTYPE html>
<html lang="en">
<head>
  <meta charset="UTF-8">
  <meta name="viewport" content="width=device-width, initial-scale=1.0">
  <title>Spaceship Game</title>
  <link rel="stylesheet" href="style.css">
</head>
<body>
  <div id="startScreen" class="screen">
    <h1>Spaceship Game</h1>
    <p>Welcome to the Spaceship game! Use arrow keys to move the spaceship.</p>
    <button id="startButton">Start Game</button>
  </div>

  <canvas id="gameCanvas"></canvas>

  <div id="gameOverScreen" class="screen">
    <h1>Game Over</h1>
    <p>You lost! Better luck next time.</p>
```

```html
    <button id="restartButton">Restart</button>
  </div>

  <script src="game.js"></script>
</body>
</html>
```

CSS Styling (style.css)

css

```css
/* General Styles */
body {
    margin: 0;
    padding: 0;
    display: flex;
    justify-content: center;
    align-items: center;
    height: 100vh;
    background-color: #111;
    color: white;
    font-family: Arial, sans-serif;
    overflow: hidden;
}

/* Screen Layout */
.screen {
```

```css
  display: none;
  text-align: center;
}

#startScreen {
  display: block;  /* Display the start screen initially */
}

button {
  padding: 10px 20px;
  background-color: #3498db;
  color: white;
  border: none;
  font-size: 18px;
  cursor: pointer;
  border-radius: 5px;
  margin-top: 20px;
}

button:hover {
  background-color: #2980b9;
}

/* Canvas styling */
canvas {
```

```
    display: block;
    background-color: #000;
    border: 2px solid #fff;
}


/* Game Over screen */
#gameOverScreen {
    display: none;  /* Hide game over screen initially */
}
```

---

3. Adding Start Screen and Game Over Screen Logic

Now, we need to connect these screens with the game logic. The game will begin when the player clicks the **"Start Game"** button, and end when the player's spaceship crashes or a similar event happens. Let's update the JavaScript file to handle these UI elements.

JavaScript Updates (game.js)

1. **Show and Hide Screens**: We need to toggle the visibility of the **start screen** and **game over screen** using JavaScript.
2. **Start the Game**: When the player clicks "Start Game," the start screen should hide, and the game canvas should appear.
3. **End the Game**: When the player loses (e.g., collides with an obstacle or reaches a game-over condition), we display the game over screen and hide the canvas.

javascript

```javascript
// Set up the canvas and context
let canvas = document.getElementById("gameCanvas");
let ctx = canvas.getContext("2d");

// Set canvas size
canvas.width = window.innerWidth;
canvas.height = window.innerHeight;

// Game elements
let spaceship = {
    x: canvas.width / 2,
    y: canvas.height / 2,
    width: 50,
    height: 50,
    speed: 5,
    dx: 0, // Movement in x direction
    dy: 0  // Movement in y direction
};

let keys = {
    ArrowUp: false,
    ArrowDown: false,
    ArrowLeft: false,
```

```
   ArrowRight: false
};


// Start and Game Over screens
let startScreen = document.getElementById("startScreen");
let gameOverScreen = document.getElementById("gameOverScreen");
let startButton = document.getElementById("startButton");
let restartButton = document.getElementById("restartButton");


// Event listeners for buttons
startButton.addEventListener("click", startGame);
restartButton.addEventListener("click", restartGame);


// Function to start the game
function startGame() {
   startScreen.style.display = "none";   // Hide start screen
   gameOverScreen.style.display = "none"; // Hide game over screen
   canvas.style.display = "block";      // Show canvas


   // Reset spaceship position
   spaceship.x = canvas.width / 2;
   spaceship.y = canvas.height / 2;
```

```
  // Start the game loop
  requestAnimationFrame(gameLoop);
}


// Function to restart the game
function restartGame() {
  spaceship.x = canvas.width / 2;
  spaceship.y = canvas.height / 2;
  startGame();
}


// Handle keyboard input
document.addEventListener("keydown", function(event) {
  if (event.key in keys) {
    keys[event.key] = true;
  }
});


document.addEventListener("keyup", function(event) {
  if (event.key in keys) {
    keys[event.key] = false;
  }
});


// Update spaceship position based on input
```

```
function updateGame() {
    if (keys.ArrowUp) spaceship.dy = -spaceship.speed;
    if (keys.ArrowDown) spaceship.dy = spaceship.speed;
    if (keys.ArrowLeft) spaceship.dx = -spaceship.speed;
    if (keys.ArrowRight) spaceship.dx = spaceship.speed;

    spaceship.x += spaceship.dx;
    spaceship.y += spaceship.dy;

    // Prevent spaceship from going out of bounds
    if (spaceship.x < 0 || spaceship.x + spaceship.width > canvas.width ||
        spaceship.y < 0 || spaceship.y + spaceship.height > canvas.height) {
        endGame();
    }

    spaceship.dx = 0;
    spaceship.dy = 0;
}

// Render game objects
function renderGame() {
    ctx.clearRect(0, 0, canvas.width, canvas.height);
    ctx.fillStyle = "white";
```

```
ctx.fillRect(spaceship.x,      spaceship.y,      spaceship.width,
spaceship.height);
}


// Main game loop
function gameLoop() {
    updateGame();   // Update game state
    renderGame();   // Render updated game state
    requestAnimationFrame(gameLoop);  // Request the next frame
}


// Function to end the game
function endGame() {
    canvas.style.display = "none";  // Hide the game canvas
    gameOverScreen.style.display = "block"; // Show the game over
screen
}
```

---

4. How It Works:

- **Start Screen**: The game begins with the **start screen** visible. The player clicks the **"Start Game"** button, which hides the start screen and shows the canvas, starting the game loop.
- **Game Over Screen**: If the spaceship hits the edges of the canvas (you can replace this with more complex game-over

logic), the **game over screen** appears, displaying a message and a **"Restart"** button to play again.

- **Canvas Display**: The canvas is initially hidden and is only shown after the player starts the game.

In this chapter, we learned how to improve the **user interface** of our game by adding essential elements like **start screens, game over screens**, and interactive **buttons**. Key takeaways:

1. **HTML Elements**: We used HTML elements such as buttons for interaction and images for enhancing the game's look and feel.

2. **CSS Styling**: We styled the UI to make the screens look appealing, including centering content and customizing buttons.

3. **Game Logic Integration**: We integrated the UI into the game flow, showing and hiding elements at appropriate times (e.g., game start, game over).

4. **UI Interactivity**: The game now responds to user input through clickable buttons, allowing players to start and restart the game.

In the next chapter, we'll dive into **collision detection** and explore how to handle interactions between game objects more effectively.

CHAPTER 13: COLLISION DETECTION: INTERACTIVITY IN YOUR GAMES

Collision detection is a crucial element of game development. It defines how different objects in the game interact with one another, such as when a character bumps into an obstacle, picks up an item, or when enemies collide with the player. This chapter will cover the basics of **collision detection**, how to implement it for simple games, and how to handle more complex collision logic.

We will focus on three key areas:

1. **Basic Collision Detection** – Understanding how to detect simple collisions between rectangular or circular objects.
2. **Building a Simple "Catch the Falling Objects" Game** – A practical example to implement collision detection in a game.
3. **Advanced Collision Detection** – Exploring more complex scenarios such as pixel-perfect collisions and using bounding boxes.

1. Basic Collision Detection Logic for Game Objects

Collision detection involves checking if two game objects overlap or touch each other. The simplest form of collision detection is for rectangular or square objects, using **axis-aligned bounding boxes (AABB)**. This type of detection compares the edges of two rectangles to see if they intersect.

Rectangle-Rectangle Collision (AABB):

To check if two rectangular objects are colliding, we can use the following conditions:

- **Object 1**: x1, y1, width1, height1
- **Object 2**: x2, y2, width2, height2

A collision occurs if:

1. The right edge of object 1 is to the right of the left edge of object 2 (x1 + width1 > x2)
2. The left edge of object 1 is to the left of the right edge of object 2 (x1 < x2 + width2)
3. The bottom edge of object 1 is below the top edge of object 2 (y1 + height1 > y2)
4. The top edge of object 1 is above the bottom edge of object 2 (y1 < y2 + height2)

If all these conditions are true, then the objects are colliding.

Example Code:

javascript

```javascript
function checkCollision(obj1, obj2) {
    return obj1.x < obj2.x + obj2.width &&
        obj1.x + obj1.width > obj2.x &&
        obj1.y < obj2.y + obj2.height &&
        obj1.y + obj1.height > obj2.y;
}
```

Circle-Circle Collision:

For objects that are circular, we use the **distance between the centers** of the circles. If the distance between the centers of two circles is less than the sum of their radii, they are colliding.

Formula:

- If distance < radius1 + radius2, then the circles are colliding.

To calculate the distance between two points (x1, y1) and (x2, y2), we use the **distance formula**:

javascript

```javascript
let distance = Math.sqrt(Math.pow(x2 - x1, 2) + Math.pow(y2 - y1, 2));
```

Example for circle collision:

javascript

```
function checkCircleCollision(circle1, circle2) {
    const distance = Math.sqrt(Math.pow(circle2.x - circle1.x, 2) +
Math.pow(circle2.y - circle1.y, 2));
    return distance < circle1.radius + circle2.radius;
}
```

2. Building a Simple "Catch the Falling Objects" Game

Now, let's build a **"Catch the Falling Objects"** game where the player controls a basket to catch falling items (like apples or balls). In this game, we will implement **collision detection** to determine when the basket catches a falling object.

HTML Structure:

html

```
<!DOCTYPE html>
<html lang="en">
<head>
    <meta charset="UTF-8">
    <meta name="viewport" content="width=device-width, initial-scale=1.0">
    <title>Catch the Falling Objects</title>
    <link rel="stylesheet" href="style.css">
```

```html
</head>
<body>
  <canvas id="gameCanvas"></canvas>

  <script src="game.js"></script>
</body>
</html>
```

CSS:

css

```css
body {
    margin: 0;
    padding: 0;
    display: flex;
    justify-content: center;
    align-items: center;
    height: 100vh;
    background-color: #f0f0f0;
    overflow: hidden;
}

canvas {
    background-color: #87CEEB;
    border: 1px solid #000;
}
```

JavaScript:

javascript

```javascript
let canvas = document.getElementById("gameCanvas");
let ctx = canvas.getContext("2d");

// Set canvas size
canvas.width = 800;
canvas.height = 600;

// Game elements
let basket = {
  x: canvas.width / 2 - 50,
  y: canvas.height - 50,
  width: 100,
  height: 20,
  dx: 0
};

let fallingObject = {
  x: Math.random() * canvas.width,
  y: 0,
  width: 30,
  height: 30,
  speed: 3
```

```javascript
};

// Player controls
document.addEventListener("keydown", function(event) {
    if (event.key === "ArrowLeft") {
        basket.dx = -5;
    }
    if (event.key === "ArrowRight") {
        basket.dx = 5;
    }
});

document.addEventListener("keyup", function(event) {
    if (event.key === "ArrowLeft" || event.key === "ArrowRight") {
        basket.dx = 0;
    }
});

// Update game elements
function update() {
    basket.x += basket.dx;

    // Prevent basket from going out of bounds
    if (basket.x < 0) basket.x = 0;
```

```javascript
    if (basket.x + basket.width > canvas.width) basket.x =
canvas.width - basket.width;

    fallingObject.y += fallingObject.speed;

    // Collision detection
    if (checkCollision(basket, fallingObject)) {
        fallingObject.y = 0;  // Reset the falling object
        fallingObject.x = Math.random() * canvas.width;
        console.log("Caught!");
    }

    if (fallingObject.y > canvas.height) {
        // Reset falling object if it falls off the screen
        fallingObject.y = 0;
        fallingObject.x = Math.random() * canvas.width;
    }
}

// Render game elements
function render() {
    ctx.clearRect(0, 0, canvas.width, canvas.height);

    // Draw the basket
    ctx.fillStyle = "brown";
```

```
  ctx.fillRect(basket.x, basket.y, basket.width, basket.height);

  // Draw the falling object
  ctx.fillStyle = "red";
  ctx.beginPath();
  ctx.arc(fallingObject.x, fallingObject.y, fallingObject.width / 2,
0, Math.PI * 2);
  ctx.fill();

  // Draw score or other UI elements (optional)
}


// Main game loop
function gameLoop() {
  update();  // Update game state
  render();  // Render game elements
  requestAnimationFrame(gameLoop);  // Request the next frame
}


// Start the game loop
gameLoop();
```

How It Works:

1. **Basket**: The player moves a basket using the left and right arrow keys. The basket is represented as a rectangle that can move horizontally.

2. **Falling Object**: An object (like an apple) falls from the top of the screen. When it reaches the bottom, it resets to fall again from a random horizontal position.

3. **Collision Detection**: We check if the basket collides with the falling object. If the object is caught by the basket, we reset its position to the top of the screen and make it fall again. This collision is checked using the checkCollision() function (from the previous section).

4. **Game Loop**: The gameLoop() function continuously updates the game state (basket movement and falling object position) and re-renders the scene.

---

3. Advanced Collision Detection for More Complex Games

While basic collision detection works well for simple games, as the complexity of your game increases (e.g., with irregular-shaped objects, multiple objects, or intricate physics), you'll need more sophisticated methods. Some advanced techniques include:

- **Pixel-perfect collision detection**: This method involves comparing the pixels of two objects to see if their opaque areas overlap. It's computationally expensive but useful for irregular shapes.

- **Bounding Circle**: For objects that don't have a simple rectangular or circular shape, you can approximate their collision box with a bounding circle that fits around the object.

- **Separating Axis Theorem (SAT)**: Used for polygonal shapes, SAT checks if there is a line (axis) along which the projections of two objects do not overlap. If such an axis exists, the objects are not colliding.

For now, the **AABB** and circle collision detection are sufficient for most beginner-level games. As you build more complex games, you'll want to explore the other techniques.

In this chapter, we learned how to implement **collision detection**, a critical element for making games interactive. We covered:

1. **Basic Collision Detection**: We implemented rectangle-rectangle and circle-circle collision logic.

2. **"Catch the Falling Objects" Game**: We applied collision detection in a practical game scenario, where the player catches falling objects with a basket.

3. **Advanced Collision Detection**: We briefly discussed more complex techniques such as pixel-perfect collision and the Separating Axis Theorem (SAT).

With this foundation, you're ready to add interactivity to your games, making them more engaging and dynamic. In the next chapter, we'll explore **game physics**, including gravity and movement mechanics, to add depth and realism to your games.

CHAPTER 14: SOUND AND MUSIC: ENHANCING THE GAME EXPERIENCE

Sound and music play a pivotal role in creating an immersive game experience. From subtle background music to impactful sound effects, audio can heighten emotional engagement, signal key actions, and provide feedback to players. This chapter will cover how to use JavaScript's built-in **Audio object** to implement sound in games, add sound effects for actions, and create a rhythm-based game that responds to sound cues.

By the end of this chapter, you will have the knowledge to enhance your game's atmosphere with music and dynamic sound effects, providing a more polished and enjoyable experience for the player.

---

1. Using JavaScript's Audio Object for Sound Effects and Background Music

JavaScript provides a simple way to add audio to a game using the Audio object. You can create sound effects and background music by initializing an Audio object with the path to the audio file (e.g., an MP3 or OGG file) and then using methods like play(), pause(), and loop() to control the audio.

Basic Audio Example:

javascript

```
// Create a new audio object for background music
let backgroundMusic = new Audio('background-music.mp3');

// Play the music
backgroundMusic.play();

// Loop the background music
backgroundMusic.loop = true;
```

This will play the background music continuously in a loop.

Creating Sound Effects:

You can use the same method to create sound effects for actions like collisions, player movements, or UI interactions.

javascript

```
// Create an audio object for a collision sound
let collisionSound = new Audio('collision-sound.mp3');

// Play the collision sound
collisionSound.play();
```

Controlling Sound Volume and Playback:

You can also adjust the volume of the audio, mute it, or control how it plays.

javascript

```
// Set volume to 50%
collisionSound.volume = 0.5;

// Pause the sound
collisionSound.pause();

// Resume the sound from where it left off
collisionSound.play();
```

2. Adding Sound Effects to Game Actions

Sound effects add dynamism to your game by providing auditory feedback when the player performs specific actions, such as scoring, jumping, colliding, or winning. Here, we will build upon the **"Catch the Falling Objects"** game from the previous chapter and add sound effects for key actions such as catching an object, missing an object, and game-over scenarios.

Updating the Catch the Falling Objects Game with Sound:

1. **Catch Sound Effect**: Play a sound when the player catches an object.

CODING GAMES WITH JAVASCRIPT

2. **Miss Sound Effect**: Play a sound when the object falls off the screen without being caught.

3. **Game Over Sound Effect**: Play a sound when the game ends.

JavaScript Updates for Sound Effects:

javascript

```javascript
// Audio files for different actions
let catchSound = new Audio('catch-sound.mp3');
let missSound = new Audio('miss-sound.mp3');
let gameOverSound = new Audio('game-over-sound.mp3');

// Update the game loop to include sound effects
function update() {
    basket.x += basket.dx;

    // Prevent basket from going out of bounds
    if (basket.x < 0) basket.x = 0;
    if (basket.x + basket.width > canvas.width) basket.x =
canvas.width - basket.width;

    fallingObject.y += fallingObject.speed;

    // Collision detection for catching the object
```

```
if (checkCollision(basket, fallingObject)) {
    catchSound.play();  // Play sound when the object is caught
    fallingObject.y = 0;  // Reset the falling object
    fallingObject.x = Math.random() * canvas.width;
    console.log("Caught!");
}

// Missed object detection (falls off the screen)
if (fallingObject.y > canvas.height) {
    missSound.play();  // Play sound when the object is missed
    fallingObject.y = 0;
    fallingObject.x = Math.random() * canvas.width;
}
}

// Game Over logic
function endGame() {
    canvas.style.display = "none";  // Hide the game canvas
    gameOverSound.play();  // Play the game over sound
    gameOverScreen.style.display = "block"; // Show the game over
screen
}
```

Explanation:

- **Catch Sound**: Plays when the player catches the falling object.
- **Miss Sound**: Plays when the object falls off the screen.
- **Game Over Sound**: Plays when the game ends (when the player misses too many objects or reaches a game over condition).

Each action now has an associated sound effect, enhancing the player's interaction and feedback during the game.

---

3. Creating a Rhythm-Based Game with Sound Feedback

A rhythm-based game relies heavily on sound cues. The player must react to the rhythm of the music, timing their actions to match the beat. This kind of game requires precise sound timing, and the use of JavaScript's setInterval() or requestAnimationFrame() allows for accurate synchronization between the game's actions and the music's rhythm.

Rhythm Game Example:

In this example, we'll build a simple rhythm-based game where a player must press a button in sync with a beat. We'll use a background track, and the player has to click at the right time to score points.

Game Concept:

- A beat is triggered at regular intervals.
- The player must click the "Hit" button when the beat occurs.
- If they click correctly, they score points.

HTML Structure:

html

```
<!DOCTYPE html>
<html lang="en">
<head>
  <meta charset="UTF-8">
  <meta name="viewport" content="width=device-width, initial-scale=1.0">
  <title>Rhythm Game</title>
  <link rel="stylesheet" href="style.css">
</head>
<body>
  <div id="gameContainer">
    <h1>Rhythm Game</h1>
    <button id="hitButton">Hit the Beat!</button>
    <p>Score: <span id="score">0</span></p>
  </div>

  <script src="game.js"></script>
</body>
```

```
</html>
```

CSS:

css

```css
body {
    font-family: Arial, sans-serif;
    text-align: center;
    padding: 50px;
    background-color: #222;
    color: white;
}

#gameContainer {
    max-width: 400px;
    margin: 0 auto;
}

button {
    padding: 20px;
    font-size: 20px;
    background-color: #3498db;
    border: none;
    color: white;
    cursor: pointer;
    border-radius: 5px;
```

```css
    transition: background-color 0.2s;
}

button:hover {
    background-color: #2980b9;
}
```

JavaScript for Rhythm Game:

javascript

```javascript
// Game variables
let score = 0;
let gamePlaying = true;

// Audio setup
let backgroundMusic = new Audio('rhythm-background-music.mp3');
let beatSound = new Audio('beat-sound.mp3');
let hitSound = new Audio('hit-sound.mp3');
let missSound = new Audio('miss-sound.mp3');

// Game UI elements
let scoreDisplay = document.getElementById("score");
let hitButton = document.getElementById("hitButton");

// Start background music
```

```javascript
backgroundMusic.loop = true;
backgroundMusic.play();

// Interval for the rhythm beat (every 1000ms = 1 second)
let beatInterval = setInterval(function() {
  if (gamePlaying) {
    beatSound.play(); // Play beat sound
    console.log("Beat!");
  }
}, 1000);

// Button click handler
hitButton.addEventListener('click', function() {
  let randomTime = Math.floor(Math.random() * 1000); // Random
time for beat accuracy
  if (randomTime > 500) {
    hitSound.play(); // Correct hit sound
    score++;
    scoreDisplay.innerText = score;
  } else {
    missSound.play(); // Missed hit sound
  }
});

// Function to stop the game after 30 seconds
```

```
setTimeout(function() {
    gamePlaying = false;
    clearInterval(beatInterval);  // Stop the beat
    alert("Game Over! Final Score: " + score);
}, 30000);  // 30 seconds of gameplay
```

How It Works:

- **Background Music**: The background music is played in a loop throughout the game.
- **Beat Sound**: A "beat" is triggered every second, and the player needs to click in sync with it.
- **Hit/Miss Detection**: The player clicks a button when they hear the beat. If they click too early or too late, they miss the beat. If they click in time, they score a point.
- **Game Timer**: After 30 seconds, the game stops, and the final score is displayed.

In this chapter, we learned how to **integrate sound** into our games using JavaScript's built-in Audio object. Key takeaways include:

1. **Basic Sound Setup**: How to play background music and sound effects using the Audio object, and how to control their playback (e.g., looping, volume).

2. **Sound Effects for Actions**: How to add sound effects for specific actions in the game (e.g., catching an object, missing a shot, or game over).

3. **Rhythm Game Example**: We created a simple rhythm-based game, where players must click in sync with beats, illustrating how to sync game events with audio cues.

With this knowledge, you can now enhance the audio experience of your games, making them more immersive and interactive. In the next chapter, we'll dive into **game physics**, where we'll focus on adding gravity, friction, and more advanced movement mechanics to your games.

CHAPTER 15: HANDLING GAME STATES: PROGRESSION AND SCORING

One of the core elements of game development is managing the **game state**—tracking where the player is in the game (e.g., starting, playing, paused, game over) and ensuring the game behaves accordingly. A game's progression, including the player's score, level, and other states (such as win or lose conditions), must be properly managed to provide a seamless and rewarding experience.

In this chapter, we'll explore:

1. **Understanding Different Game States**: How to manage various stages of gameplay.
2. **Using Variables to Track Score and Level Progress**: Keeping track of the player's performance throughout the game.
3. **Building a Score-Based Game with Different Levels**: A practical example of a game that features level progression based on the player's score, such as a simple platformer.

---

1. Understanding Different Game States

A **game state** is the current condition or phase of the game. The game will usually cycle through a few distinct states, such as:

- **Start**: The game is beginning, usually displaying a title screen and waiting for the player to begin.
- **Playing**: The game is in progress, and the player is actively engaged with the gameplay.
- **Paused**: The game is temporarily halted, usually due to player input (e.g., pressing a pause button).
- **Game Over**: The game ends, either because the player lost or they reached a goal.

Managing Game States with Variables:

To manage game states, we can use a variable (e.g., gameState) that keeps track of the current state. Based on this state, different parts of the game are executed.

javascript

```javascript
let gameState = "start"; // The game starts in the "start" state
let score = 0;
let level = 1;

function updateGameState() {
  switch(gameState) {
    case "start":
```

```
        // Display start screen
        break;
    case "playing":
        // Update game logic (e.g., player movement, score
calculation)
        break;
    case "paused":
      // Show pause menu and stop game logic
        break;
    case "gameOver":
        // Show game over screen and final score
        break;
    }
}
```

In this example, the game starts in the **"start"** state. When the player clicks a button or presses a key, the game transitions to the **"playing"** state. If the player pauses the game, it enters the **"paused"** state, and if the player loses, the game enters the **"gameOver"** state.

Transitions Between States:

You can switch between states using simple conditional checks or event listeners. For example, pressing a key could move the game from **"start"** to **"playing"**, and a button click could pause or resume the game.

javascript

```javascript
document.addEventListener("keydown", function(event) {
    if (gameState === "start" && event.key === "Enter") {
        gameState = "playing"; // Start the game when Enter is pressed
    } else if (gameState === "playing" && event.key === "p") {
        gameState = "paused"; // Pause the game when P is pressed
    } else if (gameState === "paused" && event.key === "p") {
        gameState = "playing"; // Resume the game when P is pressed
again
    }
});
```

---

2. Using Variables to Track Score and Level Progress

Tracking the player's **score** and **level** is an essential part of most games. These variables can determine the difficulty, unlock new content, and show progress.

Score and Level Variables:

You can track the score and level using simple variables. The score increases as the player performs certain actions (e.g., defeating enemies or collecting items), while the level can increase when a certain score threshold is reached.

javascript

```
let score = 0;
let level = 1;

function increaseScore(points) {
    score += points;
    if (score >= level * 100) {  // Level up when score reaches a
threshold
        levelUp();
    }
}

function levelUp() {
    level++;
    console.log("Level Up! You're now on level " + level);
}
```

Here, each time the player's score exceeds a certain threshold (100 points per level, in this case), the level increases. You can adjust the thresholds or add more complex conditions for level-ups depending on your game design.

Displaying Score and Level:

You'll likely want to show the score and level on the screen, which can be done using **DOM manipulation** or by drawing text on the canvas.

For example, with a simple HTML display:

html

```
<p>Score: <span id="score">0</span></p>
<p>Level: <span id="level">1</span></p>
```

And in the JavaScript:

javascript

```
function updateUI() {
    document.getElementById("score").innerText = score;
    document.getElementById("level").innerText = level;
}
```

This ensures that the player can always see their current score and level during the game.

---

3. Building a Score-Based Game with Different Levels (e.g., Simple Platformer)

In this section, we'll apply what we've learned by building a simple score-based game with multiple levels. For simplicity, we will create a **basic platformer** where the player needs to avoid obstacles to increase their score. As the score increases, the level progresses, and the difficulty increases (e.g., faster obstacles).

Game Concept:

- The player moves a character to avoid falling obstacles.

- For each obstacle the player avoids, they score points.
- The game advances to the next level after a certain score threshold is reached.
- At higher levels, obstacles fall faster or more frequently.

HTML Structure:

html

```
<!DOCTYPE html>
<html lang="en">
<head>
  <meta charset="UTF-8">
  <meta name="viewport" content="width=device-width, initial-scale=1.0">
  <title>Simple Platformer</title>
  <link rel="stylesheet" href="style.css">
</head>
<body>
  <h1>Simple Platformer</h1>
  <p>Score: <span id="score">0</span></p>
  <p>Level: <span id="level">1</span></p>
  <canvas id="gameCanvas"></canvas>

  <script src="game.js"></script>
</body>
```

```
</html>
```

CSS:

```
css
```

```
body {
    font-family: Arial, sans-serif;
    text-align: center;
    background-color: #eaeaea;
}

canvas {
    background-color: #333;
    border: 1px solid #000;
}
```

JavaScript for the Platformer:

```
javascript
```

```
let canvas = document.getElementById("gameCanvas");
let ctx = canvas.getContext("2d");

// Set up canvas size
canvas.width = 800;
canvas.height = 600;
```

```
// Game state and variables
let gameState = "start";
let score = 0;
let level = 1;
let player = {
    x: 100,
    y: canvas.height - 50,
    width: 50,
    height: 50,
    speed: 5
};
let obstacles = [];


// Start the game when Enter key is pressed
document.addEventListener("keydown", function(event) {
    if (gameState === "start" && event.key === "Enter") {
        gameState = "playing";
        gameLoop();  // Start game loop
    }
});


// Player movement
document.addEventListener("keydown", function(event) {
    if (event.key === "ArrowUp" && player.y > 0) {
        player.y -= player.speed;
```

```javascript
    } else if (event.key === "ArrowDown" && player.y <
canvas.height - player.height) {
        player.y += player.speed;
    } else if (event.key === "ArrowLeft" && player.x > 0) {
        player.x -= player.speed;
    } else if (event.key === "ArrowRight" && player.x <
canvas.width - player.width) {
        player.x += player.speed;
    }
});


// Generate obstacles
function generateObstacles() {
    if (Math.random() < 0.05) {   // Random chance to create an
obstacle
        let newObstacle = {
            x: canvas.width,
            y: Math.random() * (canvas.height - 50),
            width: 50,
            height: 50,
            speed: level * 2
        };
        obstacles.push(newObstacle);
    }
}
```

```javascript
// Update game state
function update() {
  if (gameState === "playing") {
    generateObstacles();

    // Move obstacles
    obstacles.forEach(function(obstacle, index) {
      obstacle.x -= obstacle.speed;
      if (obstacle.x < 0) {
        obstacles.splice(index, 1);
      }

      // Check for collision
      if (player.x < obstacle.x + obstacle.width &&
          player.x + player.width > obstacle.x &&
          player.y < obstacle.y + obstacle.height &&
          player.y + player.height > obstacle.y) {
        gameState = "gameOver";
      }
    });

    // Increase score and level
    score += 1;
    if (score >= level * 100) {
```

```javascript
      levelUp();
    }
  }
}


// Level up
function levelUp() {
  level++;
  console.log("Level Up! You're now on level " + level);
}


// Render game elements
function render() {
  ctx.clearRect(0, 0, canvas.width, canvas.height);

  // Draw player
  ctx.fillStyle = "blue";
  ctx.fillRect(player.x, player.y, player.width, player.height);

  // Draw obstacles
  obstacles.forEach(function(obstacle) {
    ctx.fillStyle = "red";
    ctx.fillRect(obstacle.x,          obstacle.y,          obstacle.width,
obstacle.height);
  });
```

```
// Update score and level
document.getElementById("score").innerText = score;
document.getElementById("level").innerText = level;
}


// Game loop
function gameLoop() {
    if (gameState === "playing") {
        update();
        render();
        requestAnimationFrame(gameLoop); // Repeat the game loop
    } else if (gameState === "gameOver") {
        alert("Game Over! Your final score is: " + score);
    }
}
```

Explanation of Platformer Game:

1. **Game States**: The game starts in the "start" state, moves to "playing" when the player presses "Enter", and enters the "gameOver" state when the player collides with an obstacle.

2. **Score and Level**: The player earns points by avoiding obstacles, and when their score reaches certain thresholds, the level increases, making the game more difficult by speeding up the obstacles.

3. **Player Movement**: The player moves using arrow keys, and obstacles are generated randomly.

4. **Collision Detection**: If the player collides with an obstacle, the game transitions to the "gameOver" state.

In this chapter, we explored how to manage **game states** (start, playing, paused, game over) using simple JavaScript variables and logic. We also learned how to track and display **score** and **level** using variables, and implemented a basic score-based game with level progression. By using these concepts, you can create more dynamic and engaging games that provide meaningful progression and feedback to players.

Next, we'll dive into **game physics** and explore how to add real-world mechanics like gravity, collision response, and object movement to your games.

CHAPTER 16: ADVANCED ANIMATION TECHNIQUES: SMOOTH AND COMPLEX MOVEMENTS

In this chapter, we'll explore more advanced animation techniques in JavaScript and CSS to make game characters and objects move smoothly and dynamically. We'll cover how to use **CSS animations in combination with JavaScript** for efficient and visually appealing animations, and dive into **advanced movement mechanics** that give game characters more complex actions, such as jumping and gravity. We'll conclude by building a **platformer** with jump and gravity mechanics, providing a practical example of how to use these techniques in real-world game development.

---

1. Using CSS Animations with JavaScript

While JavaScript offers powerful tools for animating elements, sometimes combining **CSS animations** with JavaScript can provide smoother, hardware-accelerated animations. CSS handles animations well for certain tasks, like moving elements or changing colors, because it leverages the browser's optimization engine. JavaScript, on the other hand, offers more flexibility for complex logic and interactive behavior.

CSS Keyframe Animations

CSS allows you to define animations using @keyframes. These keyframes describe the states of an element at specific points during the animation, and the browser interpolates the frames between these states.

Here's an example of a CSS animation for moving an element across the screen:

css

```
@keyframes moveRight {
    0% {
      left: 0;
    }
    100% {
      left: 100%;
    }
}


.movingElement {
    position: absolute;
    animation: moveRight 2s ease-in-out infinite;
}
```

In this example, .movingElement moves from left to right over a period of 2 seconds. You can use CSS animations for simple animations like moving elements, rotating, fading, etc.

Triggering CSS Animations from JavaScript

While CSS animations run independently of JavaScript, you can control them via JavaScript. For example, you might want to trigger an animation when a user clicks a button or a certain condition is met.

javascript

```
const element = document.querySelector(".movingElement");
element.addEventListener("click", function() {
    element.style.animation = "moveRight 2s ease-in-out"; // Trigger the animation
});
```

By combining CSS animations and JavaScript, you can create smooth, interactive animations without overloading your game loop with complex calculations.

---

2. Advanced Movement Techniques for Game Characters

For more complex movements, such as a character running, jumping, or interacting with the environment, you'll need to go beyond basic

CSS. You'll typically use JavaScript to handle movement logic, applying it to elements on a canvas or HTML elements.

Smooth Movement with RequestAnimationFrame()

To achieve smooth, continuous movement, use requestAnimationFrame(), which allows you to control the frame rate of your animations. It synchronizes the animation with the browser's rendering process, leading to smoother animations.

Here's an example of moving a character using requestAnimationFrame():

javascript

```
let player = {
    x: 100,
    y: 100,
    speed: 5,
    element: document.getElementById("player")
};


function updatePlayerPosition() {
    // Move player to the right
    player.x += player.speed;


    // Update the player's position on screen
    player.element.style.left = player.x + "px";
```

```
    // Request the next frame
    requestAnimationFrame(updatePlayerPosition);
}
```

```
// Start the animation loop
updatePlayerPosition();
```

In this example, the player's x position is updated every frame, and the element's position on the screen is adjusted. requestAnimationFrame() ensures the update happens smoothly and is optimized for the browser.

Using Velocity for More Realistic Movement

In many games, character movement is governed by **velocity**, which is the rate of change of position over time. Using velocity allows for more realistic movement, as objects can accelerate, decelerate, and move in different directions.

javascript

```
let player = {
    x: 100,
    y: 100,
    vx: 0, // horizontal velocity
    vy: 0, // vertical velocity
    speed: 5
```

```
};

function updatePlayer() {
    player.vx = player.speed;  // Set horizontal velocity to speed
    player.vy += 0.1;  // Apply gravity (vertical velocity changes over time)

    player.x += player.vx;
    player.y += player.vy;

    // Update the player's position
    player.element.style.left = player.x + "px";
    player.element.style.top = player.y + "px";

    // Check for ground collision (simple ground detection)
    if (player.y >= 500) {
        player.y = 500; // Prevent going below the ground level
        player.vy = 0;  // Reset vertical velocity (stop falling)
    }

    requestAnimationFrame(updatePlayer);  // Continue the loop
}

// Start the animation loop
updatePlayer();
```

Here, the player's horizontal velocity (vx) moves them across the screen, while gravity (vy) causes them to fall. The code detects the ground and stops the fall once the player reaches a certain y position.

---

3. Building a Platformer with Jump and Gravity Mechanics

Now that we understand the key concepts of animation and movement, let's build a **platformer** where the character can **jump** and experience **gravity**.

Game Concept:

- The player can move left and right.
- The player can jump.
- Gravity pulls the player down, and they stop falling when they hit the ground.

HTML Setup:

html

```
<!DOCTYPE html>
<html lang="en">
<head>
  <meta charset="UTF-8">
  <meta name="viewport" content="width=device-width, initial-scale=1.0">
```

```html
<title>Platformer Game</title>
<style>
  body {
    margin: 0;
    overflow: hidden;
    background-color: #87CEEB;
  }
  #gameCanvas {
    display: block;
    background-color: #228B22; /* Ground */
  }
  #player {
    position: absolute;
    width: 50px;
    height: 50px;
    background-color: #FF6347;
  }
</style>
</head>
<body>
  <div id="player"></div>
  <canvas id="gameCanvas"></canvas>
  <script src="game.js"></script>
</body>
</html>
```

JavaScript for Platformer:

javascript

```javascript
let canvas = document.getElementById("gameCanvas");
let ctx = canvas.getContext("2d");

// Set canvas size
canvas.width = 800;
canvas.height = 600;

let player = {
    x: 100,
    y: 500,
    width: 50,
    height: 50,
    vx: 0,
    vy: 0,
    speed: 3,
    gravity: 0.5,
    jumpPower: -12,
    onGround: false,
    element: document.getElementById("player")
};

let groundY = 550; // Ground level
```

```
// Handle player movement
document.addEventListener("keydown", function(event) {
    if (event.key === "ArrowLeft") {
        player.vx = -player.speed; // Move left
    } else if (event.key === "ArrowRight") {
        player.vx = player.speed; // Move right
    } else if (event.key === " " && player.onGround) { // Spacebar to jump
        player.vy = player.jumpPower;
        player.onGround = false; // Player is no longer on the ground
    }
});

// Update player position and apply gravity
function updatePlayer() {
    // Update velocity and position
    player.vy += player.gravity; // Apply gravity
    player.x += player.vx; // Update horizontal position
    player.y += player.vy; // Update vertical position

    // Collision with ground (stop falling)
    if (player.y >= groundY) {
        player.y = groundY;
        player.vy = 0;
```

```
      player.onGround = true;
  }


  // Apply movement constraints
  if (player.x < 0) player.x = 0; // Prevent moving off left side
  if (player.x > canvas.width - player.width) player.x =
canvas.width - player.width;


  // Update player element on screen
  player.element.style.left = player.x + "px";
  player.element.style.top = player.y + "px";


  // Request the next frame
  requestAnimationFrame(updatePlayer);
}


// Start the game loop
updatePlayer();
```

Explanation of Platformer Mechanics:

- **Gravity**: The player experiences gravity, which causes them to fall over time (vy += gravity). When they hit the ground, gravity is stopped, and their vertical position (y) is reset to the ground level.

- **Jumping**: When the spacebar is pressed, the player jumps. The jump is triggered by setting a negative vertical velocity (vy = -12), simulating the player being pushed upward.

- **Movement**: The player can move left and right using the arrow keys. The horizontal velocity (vx) is applied to the x position, allowing smooth movement across the screen.

- **Collision Detection**: The player stops falling once they reach the ground (y >= groundY).

In this chapter, we explored **advanced animation techniques** using CSS animations and how they can be combined with JavaScript for smoother, more efficient game animations. We learned how to create **complex movements** by applying velocity, gravity, and other forces to objects, making them more dynamic and interactive. By building a **platformer game** with jump and gravity mechanics, we learned how to integrate these animation and movement techniques to create more engaging game experiences.

Next, we will delve into **collision detection** and explore how objects can interact with each other within the game world, adding complexity and challenge to your gameplay mechanics.

CHAPTER 17: CREATING 2D GAMES WITH THE HTML5 CANVAS

In this chapter, we'll dive deeper into the **HTML5 <canvas> element**, which allows you to create complex 2D games directly in the browser. We'll cover how to use the <canvas> element to render dynamic scenes, draw backgrounds, characters, obstacles, and even handle real-time gameplay. We'll also build a simple **2D shooter game**, applying these techniques to give you a foundational understanding of creating interactive and visually rich games.

---

1. Deep Dive into the <canvas> Element for Complex Games

The <canvas> element is a powerful feature of HTML5 that allows you to draw graphics using JavaScript. It provides a resolution-dependent bitmap space where you can manipulate individual pixels and draw basic shapes, images, and even complex animations in real-time.

Canvas Setup

To get started with the <canvas> element, you first need to add it to your HTML:

html

```
<canvas id="gameCanvas" width="800" height="600"></canvas>
```

In this example, the width and height attributes define the canvas size, and id="gameCanvas" allows us to reference it in our JavaScript.

Accessing the Canvas Context

To start drawing, you need to access the **canvas context**, which provides the methods for drawing shapes, images, and text. For 2D games, you'll use the 2D context:

javascript

```javascript
let canvas = document.getElementById('gameCanvas');
let ctx = canvas.getContext('2d');
```

Here, ctx represents the **drawing context** that you'll use for all your drawing operations.

---

2. Drawing Dynamic Scenes: Backgrounds, Characters, Obstacles

Now that you have the canvas set up, let's start creating a dynamic game scene. We'll look at how to draw static and dynamic elements such as backgrounds, characters, and obstacles.

Drawing a Background

The background of your game can either be a solid color, an image, or even a scrolling texture. Here's an example of drawing a static background:

javascript

```javascript
// Draw a simple background
function drawBackground() {
    ctx.fillStyle = "#87CEEB"; // Sky blue color
    ctx.fillRect(0, 0, canvas.width, canvas.height); // Fill the entire canvas
}
```

You can also draw a **scrolling background** for games like platformers or side-scrollers:

javascript

```javascript
let backgroundX = 0;
let backgroundSpeed = 2;

function drawScrollingBackground() {
    ctx.fillStyle = "#87CEEB"; // Sky blue
    ctx.fillRect(backgroundX, 0, canvas.width, canvas.height); // Draw background
    ctx.fillRect(backgroundX - canvas.width, 0, canvas.width, canvas.height); // Draw repeated background
    backgroundX -= backgroundSpeed; // Move background to the left

    // Reset background position when it goes off screen
```

```
if (backgroundX <= -canvas.width) {
    backgroundX = 0;
  }
}
```

In this example, the background moves to the left, and when it scrolls off the screen, it resets to its original position, creating a looping effect.

Drawing Characters and Obstacles

Next, let's add characters and obstacles to the scene. You can draw shapes like rectangles, circles, and custom images:

javascript

```
// Player character
let player = {
    x: 100,
    y: 100,
    width: 50,
    height: 50,
    color: "red"
};

// Draw player
function drawPlayer() {
    ctx.fillStyle = player.color;
```

```
    ctx.fillRect(player.x, player.y, player.width, player.height);
}

// Obstacle
let obstacle = {
    x: 400,
    y: 200,
    width: 50,
    height: 50,
    color: "green"
};

// Draw obstacle
function drawObstacle() {
    ctx.fillStyle = obstacle.color;
    ctx.fillRect(obstacle.x,        obstacle.y,        obstacle.width,
obstacle.height);
}
```

In this setup, the player is a red square, and the obstacle is a green square. You can extend this by adding more complex shapes or using images for more dynamic visuals.

Moving the Player and Obstacles

For interactive elements, you'll want to update the positions of the player and obstacles in response to user input and game logic. Here's how you can update the player's position using the keyboard:

javascript

```javascript
document.addEventListener('keydown', function(event) {
    if (event.key === "ArrowLeft") {
        player.x -= 5;  // Move left
    }
    if (event.key === "ArrowRight") {
        player.x += 5;  // Move right
    }
    if (event.key === "ArrowUp") {
        player.y -= 5;  // Move up
    }
    if (event.key === "ArrowDown") {
        player.y += 5;  // Move down
    }
});
```

3. Creating a Simple 2D Shooter Game

Now that we've covered the basic setup for drawing and moving elements, let's apply these concepts to create a simple **2D shooter game**. In this game, the player will move a character and shoot bullets to destroy enemies.

Game Setup

We need the following elements:

190

- **Player ship** (a rectangular shape).
- **Bullets** (small rectangles that shoot upwards).
- **Enemies** (rectangular obstacles that the player must shoot).

javascript

```javascript
// Game variables
let player = { x: 100, y: 550, width: 50, height: 50, color: "blue" };
let bullets = [];
let enemies = [];
let gameSpeed = 1;

// Player movement
let playerSpeed = 5;
document.addEventListener("keydown", function(event) {
    if (event.key === "ArrowLeft") player.x -= playerSpeed;
    if (event.key === "ArrowRight") player.x += playerSpeed;
    if (event.key === "ArrowUp") player.y -= playerSpeed;
    if (event.key === "ArrowDown") player.y += playerSpeed;
    if (event.key === " " && bullets.length < 5) shootBullet();  // Shoot bullet on spacebar
});

// Bullet shooting
function shootBullet() {
```

```javascript
  let bullet = { x: player.x + player.width / 2 - 5, y: player.y, width:
10, height: 20, color: "yellow", speed: 7 };
  bullets.push(bullet);
}


// Draw bullets
function drawBullets() {
  bullets.forEach(function(bullet, index) {
    ctx.fillStyle = bullet.color;
    ctx.fillRect(bullet.x, bullet.y, bullet.width, bullet.height);
    bullet.y -= bullet.speed;  // Move the bullet upwards

    // Remove bullet if it goes off screen
    if (bullet.y < 0) {
      bullets.splice(index, 1);
    }
  });
}


// Generate enemies
function generateEnemies() {
  if (Math.random() < 0.01) {
    let enemy = { x: Math.random() * canvas.width, y: 0, width:
40, height: 40, color: "red", speed: 2 };
    enemies.push(enemy);
```

```
      }
   }


// Draw enemies
function drawEnemies() {
   enemies.forEach(function(enemy, index) {
      ctx.fillStyle = enemy.color;
      ctx.fillRect(enemy.x, enemy.y, enemy.width, enemy.height);
      enemy.y += enemy.speed;  // Move enemy downwards

      // Remove enemy if it goes off screen
      if (enemy.y > canvas.height) {
         enemies.splice(index, 1);
      }
   });
}


// Collision detection (bullet hit)
function checkCollisions() {
   bullets.forEach(function(bullet, bulletIndex) {
      enemies.forEach(function(enemy, enemyIndex) {
         if (bullet.x < enemy.x + enemy.width &&
            bullet.x + bullet.width > enemy.x &&
            bullet.y < enemy.y + enemy.height &&
            bullet.y + bullet.height > enemy.y) {
```

```
            // Bullet hit enemy
            bullets.splice(bulletIndex, 1);
            enemies.splice(enemyIndex, 1);
        }
    });
  });
}


// Draw everything
function drawGame() {
    ctx.clearRect(0, 0, canvas.width, canvas.height);  // Clear canvas

    drawBackground();
    drawPlayer();
    drawBullets();
    drawEnemies();

    checkCollisions();
    generateEnemies();

    requestAnimationFrame(drawGame);  // Keep looping the game
}

// Start the game loop
drawGame();
```

Explanation of Game Components:

- **Player Movement**: The player can move the ship around using the arrow keys. The ship is drawn as a blue rectangle.
- **Bullet Shooting**: When the spacebar is pressed, the player fires bullets (yellow rectangles) that move upwards.
- **Enemies**: Enemies are randomly generated at the top of the screen. They move downwards at a constant speed.
- **Collision Detection**: Bullets and enemies are checked for collisions. When a bullet collides with an enemy, both the bullet and the enemy are removed from the game.

In this chapter, we explored how to use the **HTML5 <canvas> element** to create dynamic 2D game environments. We covered drawing backgrounds, characters, and obstacles, and how to handle real-time user input to move those elements. By building a simple **2D shooter game**, we applied these techniques to create an interactive game where the player moves, shoots, and interacts with enemies.

In the next chapter, we'll dive into more advanced **game mechanics**, such as adding power-ups, game scoring, and complex physics to enhance the gameplay experience.

CHAPTER 18: INTRODUCTION TO OBJECT-ORIENTED PROGRAMMING (OOP) IN JAVASCRIPT

In this chapter, we'll introduce **Object-Oriented Programming (OOP)** in JavaScript, which is a fundamental paradigm for organizing and structuring code. By applying OOP principles, we can make our games more modular, reusable, and easier to maintain. Specifically, we'll look at **classes**, **objects**, and **methods**, and demonstrate how these concepts can help streamline game development. Finally, we'll refactor an existing game, using OOP to improve its structure and scalability.

---

1. Basics of OOP: Classes, Objects, and Methods

What is Object-Oriented Programming?

Object-Oriented Programming is a programming paradigm based on the concept of **objects**, which are instances of **classes**. In OOP, you organize your code around objects that represent real-world entities or concepts, and you encapsulate data and behavior related to those objects.

- **Class**: A blueprint or template for creating objects. It defines the properties (data) and methods (functions) that the objects created from the class will have.
- **Object**: An instance of a class. It contains real values and can access the methods defined in the class.
- **Method**: A function that is defined inside a class and is used to perform actions on the object.

Defining a Class

In JavaScript, you can define a class using the class keyword. A class typically has a **constructor**, which is a special method that runs when an object is created from the class. You can also define other methods inside the class to represent actions the object can perform.

Here's an example of how to define a simple class for a **GameObject**:

javascript

```
class GameObject {
    constructor(x, y, width, height, color) {
        this.x = x;          // Position on the x-axis
        this.y = y;          // Position on the y-axis
        this.width = width;   // Width of the object
        this.height = height; // Height of the object
```

```javascript
    this.color = color;    // Color of the object
  }


  // Method to draw the object on the canvas
  draw(ctx) {
    ctx.fillStyle = this.color;
    ctx.fillRect(this.x, this.y, this.width, this.height);

  }
}
```

In this example, the GameObject class has a constructor that initializes the object's position, size, and color. The draw method uses the canvas context (ctx) to draw the object.

Creating an Object from a Class

Once you've defined a class, you can create instances (objects) from it:

javascript

```javascript
let player = new GameObject(100, 150, 50, 50, 'blue');
let enemy = new GameObject(400, 100, 40, 40, 'red');


// Drawing the objects
player.draw(ctx);
enemy.draw(ctx);
```

Each object (player and enemy) has its own properties (e.g., position, size, color) and can call methods like draw.

---

2. Creating Reusable Code for Game Objects

One of the main advantages of OOP is the ability to reuse code. By encapsulating game entities into classes, you can easily create and manage multiple instances of the same type of object, all with different properties.

Example: Refactoring a Player and Enemy Class

Imagine we want to refactor our previous game code to use OOP principles. We can create classes for both the **Player** and **Enemy** objects, each with its own behavior and properties.

javascript

```javascript
class Player {
    constructor(x, y, width, height, color, speed) {
        this.x = x;
        this.y = y;
        this.width = width;
        this.height = height;
        this.color = color;
        this.speed = speed;
    }
```

```javascript
    move(direction) {
        if (direction === 'left') this.x -= this.speed;
        if (direction === 'right') this.x += this.speed;
        if (direction === 'up') this.y -= this.speed;
        if (direction === 'down') this.y += this.speed;
    }

    draw(ctx) {
        ctx.fillStyle = this.color;
        ctx.fillRect(this.x, this.y, this.width, this.height);
    }
}

class Enemy {
    constructor(x, y, width, height, color, speed) {
        this.x = x;
        this.y = y;
        this.width = width;
        this.height = height;
        this.color = color;
        this.speed = speed;
    }

    move() {
```

```
    this.y += this.speed; // Move downwards
  }

  draw(ctx) {
    ctx.fillStyle = this.color;
    ctx.fillRect(this.x, this.y, this.width, this.height);
  }
}
```

Creating Instances of the Player and Enemy

Now we can create multiple players and enemies and manage their behavior more easily:

javascript

```
let player = new Player(100, 300, 50, 50, 'blue', 5);
let enemy1 = new Enemy(200, 0, 40, 40, 'red', 2);
let enemy2 = new Enemy(350, 0, 40, 40, 'green', 3);


// Move player based on user input
document.addEventListener('keydown', function(event) {
    if (event.key === "ArrowLeft") player.move('left');
    if (event.key === "ArrowRight") player.move('right');
    if (event.key === "ArrowUp") player.move('up');
    if (event.key === "ArrowDown") player.move('down');
});
```

```javascript
// Game loop to draw and update game objects
function gameLoop() {
    ctx.clearRect(0, 0, canvas.width, canvas.height);  // Clear canvas

    player.draw(ctx);
    enemy1.move();
    enemy2.move();
    enemy1.draw(ctx);
    enemy2.draw(ctx);

    requestAnimationFrame(gameLoop);
}

// Start the game loop
gameLoop();
```

In this updated code, we use the Player and Enemy classes to instantiate game objects and update their behaviors. The Player can move in four directions based on keyboard input, while the Enemies move downwards on their own.

---

3. Refactoring an Existing Game Using OOP Principles

Now, let's take our earlier **2D Shooter Game** and refactor it using OOP principles. We'll create classes for the **Player**, **Bullet**, and **Enemy** objects, and organize the game logic accordingly.

Player Class

javascript

```javascript
class Player {
    constructor(x, y, width, height, color) {
        this.x = x;
        this.y = y;
        this.width = width;
        this.height = height;
        this.color = color;
        this.speed = 5;
    }

    move(direction) {
        if (direction === 'left') this.x -= this.speed;
        if (direction === 'right') this.x += this.speed;
        if (direction === 'up') this.y -= this.speed;
        if (direction === 'down') this.y += this.speed;
    }

    draw(ctx) {
        ctx.fillStyle = this.color;
```

```javascript
    ctx.fillRect(this.x, this.y, this.width, this.height);
  }
}
```

Bullet Class

javascript

```javascript
class Bullet {
  constructor(x, y, width, height, color, speed) {
    this.x = x;
    this.y = y;
    this.width = width;
    this.height = height;
    this.color = color;
    this.speed = speed;
  }

  move() {
    this.y -= this.speed;  // Bullet moves upwards
  }

  draw(ctx) {
    ctx.fillStyle = this.color;
    ctx.fillRect(this.x, this.y, this.width, this.height);
  }
}
```

Enemy Class

javascript

```javascript
class Enemy {
  constructor(x, y, width, height, color, speed) {
    this.x = x;
    this.y = y;
    this.width = width;
    this.height = height;
    this.color = color;
    this.speed = speed;
  }

  move() {
    this.y += this.speed;  // Move downward
  }

  draw(ctx) {
    ctx.fillStyle = this.color;
    ctx.fillRect(this.x, this.y, this.width, this.height);
  }
}
```

Refactoring the Game Loop

javascript

```javascript
let player = new Player(100, 300, 50, 50, 'blue');
let bullets = [];
let enemies = [];

function shootBullet() {
   let bullet = new Bullet(player.x + player.width / 2 - 5, player.y,
10, 20, 'yellow', 7);
   bullets.push(bullet);
}

function generateEnemies() {
   if (Math.random() < 0.02) {
      let enemy = new Enemy(Math.random() * canvas.width, 0, 40,
40, 'red', 2);
      enemies.push(enemy);
   }
}

function gameLoop() {
   ctx.clearRect(0, 0, canvas.width, canvas.height);

   player.draw(ctx);
   bullets.forEach(bullet => bullet.move());
   bullets.forEach(bullet => bullet.draw(ctx));
   enemies.forEach(enemy => enemy.move());
```

```
enemies.forEach(enemy => enemy.draw(ctx));

    generateEnemies();
    requestAnimationFrame(gameLoop);
}


document.addEventListener('keydown', function(event) {
    if (event.key === "ArrowLeft") player.move('left');
    if (event.key === "ArrowRight") player.move('right');
    if (event.key === "ArrowUp") player.move('up');
    if (event.key === "ArrowDown") player.move('down');
    if (event.key === " ") shootBullet();
});


gameLoop();
```

In this chapter, we introduced **Object-Oriented Programming (OOP)** in JavaScript, focusing on **classes**, **objects**, and **methods**. We demonstrated how to create reusable, modular code by encapsulating the properties and behaviors of game objects within classes. We also refactored a **2D shooter game**, applying OOP principles to improve its structure and maintainability.

By using OOP, we can create more organized, flexible, and scalable code for game development. This approach not only simplifies the management of game entities but also facilitates easier debugging and expansion as the game grows. In the next chapter, we'll explore **game physics and collision detection**, further enhancing the interactivity and realism of our games.

CHAPTER 19: HANDLING MULTIPLE GAME OBJECTS: ARRAYS AND OOP TOGETHER

In this chapter, we'll tackle the challenge of handling multiple game objects—such as characters, enemies, or obstacles—by combining the power of **arrays** with **Object-Oriented Programming (OOP)** principles. As your game expands, you'll need a way to manage many instances of the same class, like multiple enemies or power-ups. Using arrays to store these objects makes it easy to iterate through them and apply logic to each one. We'll see how arrays and OOP work together to create more dynamic and scalable game experiences.

1. Using Arrays to Manage Multiple Game Objects

Arrays are a fundamental data structure in JavaScript that allow you to store multiple values in a single variable. When it comes to games, arrays can be extremely useful for managing groups of game objects like enemies, bullets, or even platforms.

Storing Game Objects in Arrays

In the context of OOP, you can create an array that holds multiple instances of a class. For example, let's say you have a class called Enemy. Instead of creating individual variables for each enemy, you can store them in an array, making it easier to manage, update, and draw all enemies in your game.

javascript

```javascript
class Enemy {
    constructor(x, y, width, height, color, speed) {
        this.x = x;
        this.y = y;
        this.width = width;
        this.height = height;
        this.color = color;
        this.speed = speed;
    }

    move() {
        this.y += this.speed; // Move downwards
    }
```

```
draw(ctx) {
    ctx.fillStyle = this.color;
    ctx.fillRect(this.x, this.y, this.width, this.height);
  }
}
```

You can now store multiple instances of Enemy in an array:

javascript

```
let enemies = [
    new Enemy(100, 50, 40, 40, 'red', 2),
    new Enemy(200, 100, 40, 40, 'green', 3),
    new Enemy(300, 150, 40, 40, 'blue', 4)
];
```

Why Use Arrays?

Arrays allow you to easily:

- **Store multiple objects** of the same type.
- **Iterate through** all the objects in the array to perform actions on them, such as updating their positions, detecting collisions, or checking for certain game conditions.
- **Dynamically add or remove objects** (e.g., spawning new enemies or removing destroyed enemies).

2. Iterating Through Game Objects in Your Game Loop

Once your game objects are stored in an array, you need a way to update and render them continuously. In a game loop, you can **iterate through the array** and perform actions on each object, such as updating its position, detecting collisions, or drawing it on the screen.

Example: Updating Multiple Enemies

Let's continue from our previous example. We'll iterate through the enemies array in the game loop, moving each enemy and drawing them on the canvas.

javascript

```javascript
// Define the game loop function
function gameLoop() {
    ctx.clearRect(0, 0, canvas.width, canvas.height); // Clear the canvas

    // Update and draw all enemies
    enemies.forEach(enemy => {
        enemy.move(); // Move the enemy
        enemy.draw(ctx); // Draw the enemy
    });

    requestAnimationFrame(gameLoop); // Keep the loop running
```

```
}
```

```
// Start the game loop
gameLoop();
```

In this case, the forEach method iterates through each enemy in the enemies array. For each enemy, we call the move and draw methods.

Handling Other Game Objects

You can also manage other game objects in arrays, like bullets or platforms, using the same approach. For example, if you want to manage bullets fired by the player, you can store them in an array and update them in the game loop:

javascript

```
let bullets = [];

function shootBullet() {
    let bullet = new Bullet(player.x + player.width / 2 - 5, player.y,
10, 20, 'yellow', 7);
    bullets.push(bullet);
}

function gameLoop() {
    ctx.clearRect(0, 0, canvas.width, canvas.height);
```

```
// Move and draw all enemies
enemies.forEach(enemy => {
    enemy.move();
    enemy.draw(ctx);
});

// Move and draw all bullets
bullets.forEach(bullet => {
    bullet.move();
    bullet.draw(ctx);
});

requestAnimationFrame(gameLoop);
}
```

In this case:

- **Enemies** are iterated through and moved.
- **Bullets** are also iterated through and moved.
- Both enemies and bullets are drawn on the canvas.

---

3. Building a Game with Multiple Characters or Enemies

One of the most common uses of arrays in games is to handle multiple characters, enemies, or objects that have similar behaviors but differ in their positions, speeds, and other properties. In this section, we'll build a simple game with multiple enemies that the player must avoid.

Setting Up the Game

Let's start with a simple game where the player has to avoid multiple enemies. We'll use arrays to manage the enemies and check for collisions between the player and each enemy.

javascript

```javascript
// Player class
class Player {
    constructor(x, y, width, height, color) {
        this.x = x;
        this.y = y;
        this.width = width;
        this.height = height;
        this.color = color;
        this.speed = 5;
    }

    move(direction) {
        if (direction === 'left') this.x -= this.speed;
        if (direction === 'right') this.x += this.speed;
        if (direction === 'up') this.y -= this.speed;
        if (direction === 'down') this.y += this.speed;
```

```
  }

  draw(ctx) {
    ctx.fillStyle = this.color;
    ctx.fillRect(this.x, this.y, this.width, this.height);
  }
}

// Enemy class
class Enemy {
  constructor(x, y, width, height, color, speed) {
    this.x = x;
    this.y = y;
    this.width = width;
    this.height = height;
    this.color = color;
    this.speed = speed;
  }

  move() {
    this.y += this.speed; // Move downward
  }

  draw(ctx) {
    ctx.fillStyle = this.color;
```

```javascript
    ctx.fillRect(this.x, this.y, this.width, this.height);
  }
}


// Initialize player and enemies
let player = new Player(200, 300, 50, 50, 'blue');
let enemies = [
  new Enemy(100, 0, 40, 40, 'red', 2),
  new Enemy(300, 0, 40, 40, 'green', 3),
  new Enemy(500, 0, 40, 40, 'yellow', 4)
];


// Game loop
function gameLoop() {
  ctx.clearRect(0, 0, canvas.width, canvas.height); // Clear canvas

  // Move and draw player
  player.draw(ctx);

  // Move and draw all enemies
  enemies.forEach(enemy => {
    enemy.move();
    enemy.draw(ctx);
  });
```

```javascript
    // Check for collisions between player and enemies
    enemies.forEach(enemy => {
        if (isColliding(player, enemy)) {
            console.log("Game Over!");
            return;  // Exit the game loop (in a real game, you'd stop the
game here)
        }
    });

    requestAnimationFrame(gameLoop);
}

// Collision detection function
function isColliding(player, enemy) {
    return player.x < enemy.x + enemy.width &&
        player.x + player.width > enemy.x &&
        player.y < enemy.y + enemy.height &&
        player.y + player.height > enemy.y;
}

// Keyboard controls
document.addEventListener('keydown', function(event) {
    if (event.key === "ArrowLeft") player.move('left');
    if (event.key === "ArrowRight") player.move('right');
    if (event.key === "ArrowUp") player.move('up');
```

```
if (event.key === "ArrowDown") player.move('down');
});
```

```
// Start the game loop
gameLoop();
```

How It Works:

- **Player Movement**: The player can move in four directions using the arrow keys.
- **Enemy Movement**: Enemies move downward, and they are added to the game loop.
- **Collision Detection**: We use a simple collision detection function (isColliding) to check if the player collides with any enemy. If a collision occurs, the game stops and outputs "Game Over".

---

4. Expanding Your Game with Multiple Objects

Once you master the concept of handling multiple objects using arrays, you can scale your game by adding more complex logic, like:

- **Spawning enemies at random positions**.
- **Adding different types of enemies with varying speeds**.
- **Tracking multiple levels, where the difficulty increases as you progress**.

- **Implementing more complex player actions** (e.g., shooting, jumping).

In this chapter, we explored how to handle multiple game objects using **arrays** in combination with **Object-Oriented Programming (OOP)**. By storing game objects like enemies, bullets, or platforms in arrays, we can efficiently manage and manipulate them in our game loop. Iterating through arrays allows us to perform actions on all objects at once, making it easier to update their positions, detect collisions, and render them on the screen. We also built a simple game with multiple enemies and introduced collision detection.

In the next chapter, we'll dive into **game physics**, which will allow us to add more realistic movements, gravity, and interactions between objects.

CHAPTER 20: WORKING WITH APIS: ENHANCING GAMES WITH EXTERNAL DATA

In this chapter, we'll explore how to **fetch external data** from **public APIs** and use it to enhance your game mechanics. By integrating APIs into your games, you can introduce dynamic content such as random trivia questions, facts, or even live scores from external sources. This opens up a whole new world of possibilities, allowing your games to be more interactive, engaging, and ever-changing.

We'll cover:

- How to use **fetch()** to request data from public APIs.
- How to use this external data to modify game mechanics or logic.

- Integrating external data, such as trivia questions or random facts, into your games.

---

1. Fetching Data from Public APIs

JavaScript provides the fetch() method to request data from external sources. The fetch() function retrieves data from a given URL, and it returns a **Promise** that resolves with the response to the request.

Basic Example: Fetching Random Trivia Questions

Let's start by fetching trivia questions from a public trivia API. The Open Trivia Database is a free resource that offers trivia questions in various categories.

Here's how we can use fetch() to get a random trivia question:

javascript

```
function getTriviaQuestion() {
    fetch('https://opentdb.com/api.php?amount=1&type=multiple')
        .then(response => response.json())
        .then(data => {
            const question = data.results[0].question;
            const correctAnswer = data.results[0].correct_answer;
            const incorrectAnswers = data.results[0].incorrect_answers;

            displayTrivia(question, correctAnswer, incorrectAnswers);
```

```
})
   .catch(error => console.error('Error fetching trivia question:',
error));
}
```

```
function displayTrivia(question, correctAnswer, incorrectAnswers)
{
   // Display the trivia question and choices to the player
   console.log('Question:', question);
   console.log('Correct Answer:', correctAnswer);
   console.log('Choices:', [correctAnswer, ...incorrectAnswers]);
}
```

Explanation:

- We use the fetch() method to get a trivia question from the Open Trivia Database API.
- The response.json() method parses the returned JSON data.
- We then extract the trivia question and possible answers and pass them to the displayTrivia function, which logs them to the console.

You could replace console.log() with actual game logic that displays the question and answers on the screen.

---

2. Using API Data to Modify Game Mechanics

Now that we can fetch data, let's use this data to **modify game mechanics**. For example, we can use the trivia questions as part of a quiz game where the player answers multiple-choice questions.

Building a Simple Trivia Quiz Game

Let's build a simple trivia quiz game where the player answers a question fetched from an API. We'll check if the player's answer is correct and give them feedback.

javascript

```javascript
let score = 0;

function startTriviaGame() {
    getTriviaQuestion();
}

function getTriviaQuestion() {
    fetch('https://opentdb.com/api.php?amount=1&type=multiple')
        .then(response => response.json())
        .then(data => {
            const question = data.results[0].question;
            const correctAnswer = data.results[0].correct_answer;
            const incorrectAnswers = data.results[0].incorrect_answers;

            displayTrivia(question, correctAnswer, incorrectAnswers);
```

```
        promptForAnswer(correctAnswer,          [correctAnswer,
...incorrectAnswers]);
    })
    .catch(error => console.error('Error fetching trivia question:',
error));
}


function displayTrivia(question, correctAnswer, choices) {
    const questionElement = document.getElementById('question');
    questionElement.innerText = question;

    const answersElement = document.getElementById('answers');
    answersElement.innerHTML = '';

    // Shuffle answers for randomness
    choices.sort(() => Math.random() - 0.5);

    choices.forEach(choice => {
        const button = document.createElement('button');
        button.innerText = choice;
        button.addEventListener('click', () => checkAnswer(choice,
correctAnswer));
        answersElement.appendChild(button);
    });
}
```

```
function checkAnswer(selectedAnswer, correctAnswer) {
    if (selectedAnswer === correctAnswer) {
        score++;
        alert('Correct! Your score: ' + score);
    } else {
        alert('Wrong! The correct answer was: ' + correctAnswer);
    }

    // After answering, fetch a new question
    getTriviaQuestion();
}
```

Explanation:

- When the game starts, getTriviaQuestion() is called to fetch a new trivia question.
- The displayTrivia() function displays the question and its possible answers as buttons.
- When the player clicks an answer, the checkAnswer() function checks if the selected answer matches the correct answer. If so, the score increases.
- After each question, the next trivia question is fetched and displayed.

This simple mechanic allows you to enhance your game with trivia content pulled dynamically from an external API.

3. Integrating External Data Sources into Your Games

In addition to trivia questions, you can use external data to alter or enhance various aspects of your games. Here are a few ideas for integrating external data sources into your projects:

Dynamic Weather-based Game Changes

Let's say you have a game where weather affects gameplay. You can use an API like the OpenWeatherMap API to fetch weather data and adjust the game mechanics accordingly. For example, if it's raining in the game's environment, the game could slow down or introduce water-related obstacles.

javascript

```javascript
function getWeather(city) {

fetch(`https://api.openweathermap.org/data/2.5/weather?q=${city}&appid=YOUR_API_KEY&units=metric`)
    .then(response => response.json())
    .then(data => {
        const weather = data.weather[0].main;
        adjustGameForWeather(weather);
    })
    .catch(error => console.error('Error fetching weather data:', error));
```

```
}

function adjustGameForWeather(weather) {
    if (weather === 'Rain') {
        // Slow down player or add obstacles
        console.log('It's raining! Slowing down the game...');
    } else {
        // Normal game state
        console.log('The weather is clear. Game speed normal.');
    }
}
```

Explanation:

- This function fetches weather data for a given city and adjusts the game mechanics based on whether it's raining or clear.

- This could be extended to include different types of weather, each affecting the game in unique ways.

Using Leaderboards from an API

If you want to include high scores or leaderboards in your game, you could fetch data from a public leaderboard API. For example, the Spoonacular API provides access to a wide range of game-related data. You could fetch the top players' scores from the server and display them in a leaderboard section of your game.

4. Challenges and Considerations

While APIs provide a powerful way to enhance your games, there are some challenges and considerations to keep in mind:

- **Rate Limits**: Many APIs have rate limits that restrict how many requests you can make per hour or per day. Be mindful of these limits when designing your game, especially if it makes frequent API calls.

- **Error Handling**: External APIs can go down, or the request might fail. Always include error handling to deal with issues like timeouts or missing data.

- **CORS (Cross-Origin Resource Sharing)**: Some APIs may require special headers to access them from the browser due to security restrictions. If you encounter issues with CORS, you may need to use a server-side proxy.

In this chapter, we learned how to integrate **external data** into our games using public APIs. We explored how to use the fetch() function to retrieve data and modify our game mechanics based on that data. We built a simple **trivia quiz game** that uses an API to fetch trivia questions and answers, and we discussed other ways to use external data, such as **weather effects** or **leaderboards**.

Integrating APIs allows you to add dynamic content to your games, making them more interactive and engaging for players. In the next chapter, we'll dive into **game physics** to add even more depth to our game mechanics.

CHAPTER 21: BUILDING A WEB-BASED GAME: DEPLOYING TO THE INTERNET

In this chapter, we'll walk through the process of taking your game from development to deployment, making it accessible on the **internet** for others to play. We'll cover the following topics:

1. **Setting up a basic web server with Node.js**: Learn how to serve your game files (HTML, CSS, JavaScript) using a Node.js server.

2. **Hosting your game online for others to play**: We'll cover the basics of hosting your game on a public server.

3. **Creating a simple multiplayer game with real-time interactions**: Introduce real-time interactions by using WebSockets to allow players to interact with each other in the game.

1. Setting Up a Basic Web Server with Node.js

To serve your game over the internet, you'll first need to set up a **web server**. Node.js is an excellent tool for this purpose. It allows you to run JavaScript code on the server side, which makes it ideal for building web applications and games.

Installing Node.js

If you don't have Node.js installed yet, you can download and install it from the official website. After installation, verify it by running the following command in your terminal:

bash

node -v

This will print the version of Node.js installed on your machine.

Setting Up a Simple Server with Express

Once Node.js is installed, you can use **Express**, a minimal web server framework, to serve your game files. Let's walk through setting up a simple Express server.

1. **Initialize your project**: Open a terminal in the root folder of your game project and run the following command to create a package.json file (if you don't already have one):

   bash

npm init -y

2. **Install Express**: To use Express, install it via npm:

bash

npm install express

3. **Create the server**: In the root folder of your project, create a file named server.js. This will contain the code to set up the server.

javascript

```
const express = require('express');
const path = require('path');

const app = express();
const PORT = process.env.PORT || 3000;

// Serve static files (HTML, CSS, JS)
app.use(express.static(path.join(__dirname, 'public')));

// Serve the game index.html
app.get('/', (req, res) => {
```

```
    res.sendFile(path.join(__dirname, 'public', 'index.html'));
});

app.listen(PORT, () => {
    console.log(`Server          is          running          on
http://localhost:${PORT}`);
});
```

Explanation:

- express.static() serves static files like images, stylesheets, and JavaScript files from the public directory.
- app.get() defines a route to serve the index.html file when users visit your site.
- The server listens on port 3000 by default.

4. **Directory Structure**: Make sure your game files (HTML, CSS, JS) are placed in a public directory. Here's an example of how the folder structure might look:

bash

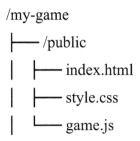

```
/my-game
├── /public
│   ├── index.html
│   ├── style.css
│   └── game.js
```

└── server.js

5. **Start the server**: In the terminal, run the following command to start the server:

bash

node server.js

Your game should now be accessible in a browser at http://localhost:3000.

---

2. Hosting Your Game Online for Others to Play

Once you've set up the local server, the next step is to **host your game online** so that other players can access it from anywhere. There are several ways to deploy your game, including free options that are simple to use.

Option 1: Using GitHub Pages for Static Games

If your game is purely static (only HTML, CSS, and client-side JavaScript), you can use **GitHub Pages** to host it for free.

1. **Create a GitHub repository**: Create a new repository on GitHub and push your project's code to the repository.

2. **Enable GitHub Pages**: Go to your repository's settings and scroll down to the "GitHub Pages" section. Choose the main

branch (or whichever branch contains your game) as the source and save.

3. **Access the game**: GitHub Pages will provide you with a link to your live game. It might look something like https://username.github.io/repository-name/.

Option 2: Deploying with Heroku (for Server-Side Games)

If your game uses a **server-side component** (such as Node.js), you'll need a platform like **Heroku** to host your game. Heroku offers free hosting for small applications.

1. **Sign up for a Heroku account** at heroku.com.
2. **Install the Heroku CLI**: Download and install the Heroku CLI from the Heroku website.
3. **Prepare for deployment**: In your project folder, create a Procfile (no file extension) with the following content:

makefile

web: node server.js

4. **Deploy the game**: Run the following commands from your terminal:

bash

git init

git add .

git commit -m "Initial commit"

heroku create

git push heroku master

This will push your game to Heroku and make it available at a URL like https://your-app-name.herokuapp.com/.

---

3. Creating a Simple Multiplayer Game with Real-Time Interactions

To make your game more interactive, you can add multiplayer functionality. For this, you'll use **WebSockets,** a protocol that allows real-time, two-way communication between the server and the client. We'll use the **Socket.io** library, which simplifies WebSocket communication in Node.js.

Setting Up WebSockets with Socket.io

1. **Install Socket.io**: First, install Socket.io by running:

   bash

   npm install socket.io

2. **Create a Basic Multiplayer Server**: Modify your server.js to include the Socket.io server.

javascript

```javascript
const express = require('express');
const http = require('http');
const socketIo = require('socket.io');
const path = require('path');

const app = express();
const server = http.createServer(app);
const io = socketIo(server);

const PORT = process.env.PORT || 3000;

app.use(express.static(path.join(__dirname, 'public')));
app.get('/', (req, res) => {
    res.sendFile(path.join(__dirname, 'public', 'index.html'));
});

// Handle player connections
io.on('connection', (socket) => {
    console.log('A user connected');

    // Example of emitting data to the client
    socket.emit('message', 'Welcome to the game!');
```

```
// Handle disconnection
socket.on('disconnect', () => {
    console.log('A user disconnected');
});
});

server.listen(PORT, () => {
    console.log(`Server is running on
http://localhost:${PORT}`);
});
```

Explanation:

- http.createServer(app) creates an HTTP server to run Express with WebSocket support.
- socketIo(server) initializes Socket.io on top of the server.
- When a user connects, the server sends a welcome message to the client.

3. **Client-side Socket.io**: In the public folder, you'll need to modify the game's JavaScript to use Socket.io to communicate with the server. First, include the Socket.io client library in your index.html:

html

```html
<script src="/socket.io/socket.io.js"></script>
```

Then, in your game.js file, add the following code:

javascript

```
const socket = io();

// Listen for a message from the server
socket.on('message', (message) => {
    console.log(message);  // Display the welcome message
});

// Example: Emit a message to the server when a player
moves
function playerMoved(playerData) {
    socket.emit('playerMove', playerData);
}
```

4. Testing and Final Adjustments

Once your game is hosted and WebSockets are working, it's time to test the multiplayer functionality. Here's what you should check:

- **Multiple Clients**: Open your game in multiple browser windows or tabs to test real-time interactions.
- **Game Logic**: Ensure that game mechanics like player movement or interactions work smoothly across clients.

- **Latency and Performance**: Monitor latency issues and make performance optimizations if needed.

In this chapter, we covered the steps required to deploy your game to the internet, making it accessible for others to play. We started by setting up a basic **Node.js web server** with Express to serve your game files, and then we looked at **hosting your game online** using platforms like GitHub Pages and Heroku. Finally, we introduced **Socket.io** to create a simple multiplayer game with real-time player interactions.

By the end of this chapter, you'll have a live, interactive game that others can play, and you'll have learned the fundamentals of server-side game deployment and real-time multiplayer mechanics.

In the next chapter, we'll explore **game physics**, adding more realism and depth to your game mechanics.

CHAPTER 22: GAME DESIGN PRINCIPLES: CREATING ENGAGING GAMEPLAY

In this chapter, we'll focus on the **art of game design**, exploring key principles that will help you create **engaging, fun, and challenging gameplay**. These principles are essential for building a game that players want to keep coming back to. We'll break down the key aspects of game design, including **balance**, **challenge**, and **rewards**, and show you how to apply them while designing your own games.

By the end of this chapter, you'll understand how to design games that keep players hooked and learn how to build a simple **puzzle or strategy game** that exemplifies these principles.

---

1. Key Game Design Principles: Balance, Challenge, and Rewards

A good game is not just about great visuals or a cool idea. It's about creating a **balanced experience** where players are constantly challenged but not frustrated, and where they are rewarded for their progress. Here are the three pillars of engaging game design:

Balance

Balance refers to how well the game mechanics and difficulty level work together to create a fair and enjoyable experience. An unbalanced game can be frustrating or boring—if it's too easy, players lose interest quickly, and if it's too difficult, they may give up.

- **Difficulty Curve**: Games should gradually introduce more complex challenges to help players feel a sense of progression. The **difficulty curve** should start easy to let new players learn the game mechanics and then slowly ramp up the challenge as they progress.

- **Game Mechanics**: Every aspect of the game, from movement to combat to puzzle-solving, should be balanced. If one mechanic is too powerful or too weak, it can disrupt the entire experience.

Challenge

A key part of any game is **challenge**—the obstacles or tasks that players need to overcome. Challenge keeps players engaged by testing their skills, knowledge, or reflexes.

- **Skill vs. Luck**: Good games typically balance skill-based challenges (e.g., puzzles, strategic decision-making, or dexterity) with an element of chance (e.g., random number generation, chance-based rewards).

- **Progressive Challenge**: As players get better, the game should adapt to keep them engaged. The challenge should increase over time but at a pace that feels fair. If the game gets harder too quickly, players may feel overwhelmed and quit. If it's too easy, they may get bored.

- **Feedback Loops**: Players need feedback to understand how they're performing. Positive feedback reinforces good actions, while negative feedback shows areas for improvement.

Rewards

Rewards keep players motivated to keep playing. They provide a sense of accomplishment, offer tangible benefits (like upgrades or new levels), and reinforce the feeling of progression.

- **Immediate vs. Long-term Rewards**: Immediate rewards, such as points, power-ups, or visual feedback, give players satisfaction in the short term. Long-term rewards, such as new levels or game modes, keep players coming back to see what comes next.

- **Intrinsic vs. Extrinsic Motivation**: Intrinsic rewards come from within (e.g., the satisfaction of solving a puzzle), while extrinsic rewards are external (e.g., points or prizes). Balancing both types of rewards can keep the gameplay experience fulfilling.

---

2. Building User-Friendly Games That Keep Players Engaged

An engaging game isn't just about balancing the right mechanics—it's also about **making the game accessible** and enjoyable for the player. Here are some best practices for creating user-friendly games:

Intuitive Controls and Interface

- **Simple and Clear Controls**: Ensure that your game's controls are easy to understand and don't overwhelm players. For example, in a puzzle game, simple mouse clicks or drag-and-drop mechanics are easy to pick up, while in a platformer, using the arrow keys for movement and space for jumping is intuitive.
- **Visual Feedback**: Players should know when they've done something right (success) or wrong (failure) with clear visual cues (like flashing buttons or animations) and audio cues (like sounds or music).
- **Accessible UI**: Keep the **user interface (UI)** simple and non-distracting. Make sure buttons, menus, and other elements are easy to find and use. Provide options to adjust volume, game speed, or difficulty if applicable.

Progression and Clear Goals

- **Set Clear Objectives**: Let players know what they need to achieve. For example, in a puzzle game, set clear goals like "reach level 10" or "collect all items". This gives players a sense of direction.

- **Meaningful Progression**: Allow players to see their progress through a visual indicator (like a progress bar) or with unlocking new features or levels. If players feel like they are moving forward, they are more likely to stay engaged.

Avoiding Frustration

- **Fair Difficulty**: Challenge should feel rewarding, not punishing. Avoid making players repeat tasks over and over for minor mistakes. Provide checkpoints or save points, and ensure that failure is not overly harsh.

- **Tutorial and Learning Curve**: Provide a tutorial for players to get used to the mechanics without overwhelming them. Let them learn as they play rather than bombarding them with too much information upfront.

---

3. Designing a Simple Puzzle or Strategy Game

Now that we have a solid understanding of game design principles, let's apply them by designing a **simple puzzle or strategy game**. We'll focus on a **number-based puzzle game** where players need to reach a target number by combining smaller numbers. This example will demonstrate how to create a fun, balanced experience with increasing challenge and rewarding feedback.

Game Concept: Number Merge Puzzle

- **Objective**: The player is presented with a 4x4 grid filled with random numbers. The player can combine adjacent numbers (e.g., 2 + 2 = 4, 4 + 4 = 8) to reach higher values, with the ultimate goal of reaching a target number (e.g., 2048).

- **Challenge**: As the player combines numbers, the grid fills up, and the player must make strategic decisions to avoid running out of space or moves.

- **Rewards**: Players receive a score based on the numbers they combine. New levels or bonus moves are unlocked when players reach milestones.

Game Design Breakdown

- **Difficulty Curve**: Start with an easy grid (smaller numbers, fewer obstacles) and slowly introduce more challenging grids (larger numbers, more complex combinations).

- **Balance**: Ensure the combinations are possible but not too easy. Provide enough opportunities for players to strategize, but don't make it so hard that it feels impossible.

- **Reward System**: Give players a sense of accomplishment with every successful combination. The game could include visual effects, sounds, and level progression that rewards players for reaching new number milestones.

Gameplay Flow:

1. **Start Screen**: The player is presented with a clean grid and a target number (e.g., 2048). A simple tutorial explains the controls.
2. **Gameplay Loop**: The player makes moves by combining numbers. New numbers appear randomly on the grid, increasing the challenge.
3. **End of Game**: The game ends when the player either reaches the target number or runs out of moves or space.

Implementation Considerations:

- **Input Handling**: Use keyboard or mouse events for grid interactions (e.g., clicking or pressing arrow keys to merge numbers).
- **Progress Feedback**: Show the player's score and progress toward the target number. Offer a retry or restart option at the end of each round.
- **Balancing Mechanics**: Ensure that numbers appear at a rate that keeps the player engaged but doesn't overwhelm them. Players should always feel like they have a chance to win, even if it's a slim one.

In this chapter, we explored the key **game design principles** that make gameplay engaging: **balance**, **challenge**, and **rewards**. We discussed how to keep your games **user-friendly** by focusing on intuitive controls, clear goals, and fair difficulty. Finally, we applied these principles by designing a **number merge puzzle game**, which incorporates progression, strategic decision-making, and rewards to keep players engaged.

Understanding and applying these principles will help you create games that are not only fun but also addictive in the best way. In the next chapter, we'll dive into **game testing** to ensure your game is smooth, bug-free, and ready for players to enjoy.

CHAPTER 23: DEBUGGING AND OPTIMIZING YOUR GAME CODE

In this chapter, we'll focus on the crucial skills of **debugging** and **optimizing** your game code. As you build more complex games, you'll inevitably encounter bugs or performance issues. Knowing how to **identify, troubleshoot, and fix** these problems efficiently is essential to delivering a smooth and enjoyable gaming experience. We'll also discuss strategies for **optimizing your game** to improve performance, reduce loading times, and enhance the overall user experience.

By the end of this chapter, you'll have a solid understanding of common debugging techniques, how to optimize your JavaScript code, and how to refactor your game for improved efficiency and readability.

---

1. Common JavaScript Debugging Techniques

Debugging is the process of finding and fixing bugs (errors) in your code. When building games, errors can arise from a variety of sources—syntax errors, logic errors, or issues related to user input. Fortunately, there are several tools and strategies you can use to make the debugging process faster and more effective.

Console Logs

One of the most basic but powerful debugging techniques in JavaScript is the use of console.log() statements. This allows you to print out values, track the flow of your program, and understand what's happening at different points in your game.

- **Use console.log() to Inspect Variables**: If something isn't working as expected, log the values of key variables. For example:

javascript

```
let playerScore = 10;
console.log('Player Score:', playerScore);
```

- **Track Function Calls**: You can also log function calls to ensure they're being invoked correctly:

javascript

```
function startGame() {
    console.log('Game has started!');
}
```

- **Array and Object Inspection**: You can log the contents of arrays or objects to check if their values are what you expect:

javascript

```
let gameBoard = [0, 1, 2];
console.log('Game board:', gameBoard);
```

Note: While console.log() is incredibly useful for small-scale debugging, it can clutter the output when your game grows more complex. Be sure to remove or comment out unnecessary logs once you've resolved issues.

Breakpoints

Breakpoints allow you to **pause the execution** of your code at specific lines, so you can inspect variables and the state of your game at that point in time. This is useful for **step-by-step debugging**.

- **How to Use Breakpoints**: In most modern browsers, you can open the **Developer Tools** (usually F12 or right-click > "Inspect") and navigate to the **Sources** tab. There, you can find your JavaScript files and click on the line number where you want to set a breakpoint.

- **Stepping Through Code**: Once a breakpoint is hit, you can use the "step over" and "step into" buttons to move through the code one line at a time, inspecting the state of variables and game objects as you go.

Breakpoints allow you to pause and inspect what's happening in real-time, which is especially useful in more complicated logic or animations.

Error Messages

When something goes wrong in JavaScript, the browser's **console** typically outputs an **error message**. Understanding and interpreting these error messages is key to debugging:

- **Syntax Errors**: These usually appear when there's a typo or missing punctuation (e.g., missing semicolon or unmatched parentheses). The error message will often specify the exact line number where the error occurs.

- **Reference Errors**: Occur when trying to use an undefined variable or function. The error message will indicate what is undefined and where the issue is.

- **Type Errors**: These happen when an operation is performed on an incompatible type (e.g., trying to call a function on an undefined value). The error message will tell you what types are involved.

Be sure to carefully read through error messages, as they often include valuable information about where and why your game isn't behaving as expected.

2. Optimizing Code for Better Performance

Once you've debugged your game and it's functioning as expected, the next step is to **optimize** it for better performance. This can improve load times, frame rates, and overall responsiveness.

Efficient DOM Manipulation

When working with JavaScript in a game, you may need to manipulate the DOM (Document Object Model) to update elements on the screen. However, **frequent DOM manipulation** can slow down your game's performance, especially if there are a lot of elements being updated in real-time (e.g., in animation or fast-paced games).

- **Batch DOM Updates**: Instead of making frequent updates to the DOM (e.g., changing one element at a time), try to **batch changes** and update them all at once. This can be done by creating a "virtual" DOM in JavaScript and updating the real DOM once, reducing the number of reflows and repaints.

- **Minimize Reflows and Repaints**: A **reflow** occurs when the browser recalculates the layout of the page, and a **repaint** happens when an element's appearance changes. Both can be costly in terms of performance. To optimize, avoid modifying styles (e.g., width, height, margin) and layout properties repeatedly.

Reducing Unnecessary Computation

If your game involves complex calculations (e.g., physics simulations, AI), make sure you're not doing unnecessary work.

- **Memoization**: This technique stores the results of expensive function calls and reuses the result when the same inputs occur again. This can dramatically speed up your game if you're performing repetitive calculations.

javascript

```javascript
let cache = {};
function expensiveCalculation(x) {
    if (x in cache) return cache[x];
    let result = x * 2; // Example expensive calculation
    cache[x] = result;
    return result;
}
```

- **Lazy Evaluation**: If you have functions or events that only need to be computed once certain conditions are met, defer their execution until absolutely necessary.

Optimizing Loops and Animations

Game loops and animations can become a performance bottleneck if not handled efficiently. Here are some tips to optimize them:

- **requestAnimationFrame()**: Instead of using setInterval() or setTimeout() for animations, use requestAnimationFrame() for smoother, more efficient frame updates. This method synchronizes the frame updates with the browser's rendering cycle, making animations smoother and less resource-intensive.

javascript

```
function gameLoop() {
    // Update game state and redraw the scene here
    requestAnimationFrame(gameLoop);  // Call the game
loop again
}
requestAnimationFrame(gameLoop);  // Start the game loop
```

- **Optimize Collision Detection**: If your game involves many objects interacting, try to **optimize collision detection algorithms**. Instead of checking every object against every other object (which can be slow), consider using spatial partitioning (e.g., grid-based collision detection) or simpler bounding-box checks.

---

3. Refactoring to Improve Game Efficiency and Readability

As your game grows more complex, your code can become difficult to manage and maintain. **Refactoring** is the process of restructuring code to improve its readability, reduce duplication, and improve efficiency without changing its external behavior.

Modularize Your Code

One of the best ways to keep your codebase clean and manageable is by breaking your code into **modular, reusable components**. For example:

- **Functions and Methods**: Instead of writing lengthy, monolithic blocks of code, break your game logic into small, self-contained functions that handle specific tasks (e.g., updating the score, checking for collisions, or drawing an object).

- **Objects and Classes**: Use **object-oriented programming (OOP)** principles to organize related functionality into classes. For example, a Player class might handle everything related to the player's movement, health, and score.

Avoiding Redundancy

- **DRY Principle**: The "Don't Repeat Yourself" principle means that you should avoid duplicating code. If you find yourself writing the same logic in multiple places, extract it into a function or method. This makes your code easier to maintain and debug.

Code Comments and Documentation

- **Comment Your Code**: Even though JavaScript can be quite readable, providing clear comments explaining complex logic will help you (and others) understand the code when revisiting it later.

- **Consistent Naming Conventions**: Use clear and consistent variable and function names. For example, use getPlayerScore() instead of something vague like score().

In this chapter, we explored the key skills of **debugging** and **optimizing** your game code. We covered common **debugging techniques** such as using console.log(), breakpoints, and reading error messages. We also discussed strategies for improving your game's **performance**, such as efficient DOM manipulation, reducing unnecessary computation, and optimizing loops and animations. Finally, we talked about the importance of **refactoring** your code to make it more modular, readable, and efficient.

By mastering these techniques, you'll be able to troubleshoot issues, optimize performance, and keep your game code clean and maintainable as you build more complex projects.

In the next chapter, we'll explore **game testing**—ensuring your game is polished, bug-free, and ready for release.

CHAPTER 24: CREATING YOUR FINAL PROJECT: A COMPLETE JAVASCRIPT GAME

In the final chapter, we'll tie everything you've learned throughout this book into a **complete, fully functional game**. This chapter will walk you through the process of **planning, coding, and testing** a final game project that combines all the skills and concepts you've mastered. Whether you're building a simple puzzle game, an action-packed platformer, or a strategy game, this chapter will provide a comprehensive, step-by-step guide to help you see your ideas come to life and share your game with the world.

By the end of this chapter, you will have completed your **final JavaScript game project**, learned how to **test** it for quality assurance, and understand how to **share it with others**—whether by publishing it on your website or distributing it online for others to enjoy.

---

1. Using Everything Learned to Build a Complete, Fully Functional Game

You've already gained a solid understanding of **JavaScript basics**, **game development principles, animations, user input**, and more.

Now it's time to put all that knowledge into a single, cohesive project.

Choosing Your Game Type

First, decide on the **type of game** you want to create. Here are some options based on your interests and the skills you've learned:

- **Puzzle Game**: A simple game where players need to solve challenges to progress. Examples include number games, word games, or match-3 games.
- **Platformer**: A side-scrolling game where players control a character jumping over obstacles, collecting items, or fighting enemies.
- **Shooter Game**: A 2D or 3D game where players shoot at enemies or objects to score points.
- **Strategy Game**: A game that requires planning and tactics, such as a tower defense or card game.
- **Arcade Game**: A fast-paced game with high scores, such as a racing or endless runner game.

Choose a concept that excites you, but also consider its complexity based on your current skill level. A good final project should challenge you but not overwhelm you.

Planning Your Game

Before jumping into the code, **plan** out your game. This helps ensure that the final product is cohesive and functional.

1. **Define the Game Mechanics**: What is the player's goal? What actions can the player take? How do they interact with the game world? Example:
   - **Objective**: Collect all the coins while avoiding enemies.
   - **Player Actions**: Use arrow keys to move, space to jump.
   - **Game Progression**: Increase difficulty as the player collects more coins (e.g., faster enemies, more obstacles).

2. **Outline the Game Flow**: Define the different stages of the game—**start screen, gameplay, game over screen**, etc. Plan how players will navigate through these stages.

3. **Create the Assets**: If your game involves images, sounds, or other media, prepare these assets in advance. Whether you're using custom-made images or free online resources, having your assets ready will save time.

4. **Sketch the Layout**: If your game involves a graphical interface (such as a platformer or shooter), sketch out how you want the screen to look. Where will the player's score appear? How will the game world be divided into levels or stages?

Coding the Game

Start coding your game based on your plan. Break the game into small chunks of work to avoid feeling overwhelmed:

1. **Set Up the Basic Structure**: Create the HTML, CSS, and JavaScript files for your game.

    o **HTML**: Set up the game container, canvas, or divs for displaying game content.

    o **CSS**: Style your game screen and game elements, including positioning and animations.

    o **JavaScript**: Start with game initialization, defining variables for player health, score, level, etc.

2. **Implement Core Mechanics**: Begin with the game mechanics that drive the gameplay (e.g., movement, collision detection, scoring system).

    o If it's a platformer, start with player movement and gravity mechanics.

    o For a puzzle game, implement the logic for moving pieces or solving puzzles.

3. **Create Game Entities**: Write code to handle all the **game objects** (e.g., player, enemies, obstacles, items) using functions, objects, or classes.

    o Use classes for complex entities like enemies or items. You can use inheritance for different types of enemies (e.g., flying, walking).

4. **Implement Game Loop**: Set up the game loop using requestAnimationFrame(), where you'll update the game state, handle user input, and redraw the screen.

javascript

```
function gameLoop() {
  updateGame();
  drawGame();
  requestAnimationFrame(gameLoop);
}
requestAnimationFrame(gameLoop);
```

5. **Add Interactivity**: Implement event listeners to handle user input (e.g., keyboard or mouse actions). For example, listening for key presses in a platformer or clicking on buttons in a puzzle game.

javascript

```
document.addEventListener('keydown', (event) => {
  if (event.key === 'ArrowLeft') {
    movePlayerLeft();
  }
});
```

6. **Design the User Interface**: Add **scoreboards**, **menus**, and **game-over screens**. Make sure the UI is clear and responsive, especially if the player needs to access settings or restart the game.

7. **Test and Debug**: Continuously test your game as you develop. Use the **debugging techniques** from the previous chapter to fix any errors and improve performance. Playtest your game to ensure it's enjoyable and balanced.

---

2. Step-by-Step Guide to Planning, Coding, and Testing Your Final Project

Step 1: Game Planning

- **Game Concept**: Choose your game type and define core mechanics (e.g., a puzzle game where players match pairs of numbers).
- **Sketch Layout**: Draw out the game screen and plan where each element (score, player, obstacles) will appear.
- **Create Assets**: Prepare any necessary images, sounds, or animations that will be used in your game.

Step 2: Game Coding

- **Set Up Project Files**: Create separate files for HTML, CSS, and JavaScript.
- **Write Game Logic**: Start with core gameplay mechanics. Define game variables (e.g., score, level, health), and create functions to handle player actions.
- **Create Game Objects**: Use JavaScript classes for reusable game elements (e.g., player, enemies).
- **Set Up Game Loop**: Create a continuous loop that updates and redraws the game state.
- **Handle User Input**: Implement keyboard or mouse input to control the game.

Step 3: Testing

- **Playtesting**: Play your game multiple times to ensure the mechanics work as intended. Does the game feel balanced? Is it too easy or too hard?
- **Bug Fixing**: Use console.log() and breakpoints to identify and fix bugs in the game code.
- **Performance Testing**: Check if your game runs smoothly. Optimize any slow areas using techniques like reducing DOM manipulations or improving logic.

Step 4: Refining

- **Polish the Game**: Add sound effects, smooth animations, and any additional features to improve the user experience.
- **Improve the UI**: Ensure your menus and buttons are intuitive and easy to use.

---

3. Wrapping Up and Sharing Your Game with the World

Once your game is complete, it's time to share it with others. Here's how you can showcase your project:

Publish Online

1. **Host on a Website**: You can use **GitHub Pages**, **Netlify**, or **Vercel** to host your game for free. Simply upload your game files, and you'll get a URL where anyone can play your game.
2. **Publish on Game Platforms**: If you want to share your game with a wider audience, consider publishing it on game platforms like **Itch.io** or **Kongregate**.
3. **Social Media**: Share your game on social media to get feedback and invite others to play. Platforms like Twitter, Reddit (in subreddits like r/gamedev), and game development forums can help you gain visibility.

Creating Documentation and Tutorials

If you want to make your game accessible to others or share how you built it, consider creating a **README file** or a **tutorial** that explains:

- The gameplay mechanics
- How to play
- What technologies and tools were used
- Any challenges you faced during development

In this final chapter, we walked through the process of creating a complete, fully functional game using everything you've learned. We covered how to **plan** your game, break it into manageable parts, **code** the core mechanics, and **test** your game for bugs and performance issues. Finally, we explored ways to **share** your game with the world, whether by publishing it on a personal website, using game platforms, or engaging with online communities.

Congratulations on reaching the end of this journey! By now, you've gained the skills to not only build JavaScript games but also to think critically about game design, debugging, and optimization. The world of game development is vast, and this is just the beginning. Keep experimenting, building, and sharing your creations with others.